ROMAN BRITAIN

Current and forthcoming titles in the Classical World Series

Classical World Series

ROMAN BRITAIN

Stephen Hill
and
Stanley Ireland

Bristol Classical Press

General Editor: John H. Betts
Series Editor: Michael Gunningham

First published in 1996 by
Bristol Classical Press
an imprint of
Gerald Duckworth & Co. Ltd
61 Frith Street
London W1V 5TA

Reprinted 1999

A catalogue record for this book is available
from the British Library

ISBN 1-85399-140-6

Printed in Great Britain by
Antony Rowe Ltd

Contents

List of Figures and Tables

Drawings for Figs. 1-2, 4-12, 14-16, 19 and 21 are by Richard Bayliss.
Drawings for Figs. 3, 13, 17-18, 20 and 22 are by Stephen Hill.

Note

Chapters 1, 2, 4, 6 and 8 were written by Stephen Hill.
Chapters 3, 5 and 7 were written by Stanley Ireland.

Acknowledgements

Stephen Hill would like to acknowledge here his great debt to Michael Gunningham, his long-suffering editor, and to his co-author for enduring the delays in the presentation of the manuscript of this volume. He would also like to thank Richard Bayliss who produced many of the illustrations and Dan Smith for much help in the final stages of text preparation after he broke his wrist.

1	Aldborough	Isurium Brigantum
2	Brough-on-Humber	Petuaria
3	Caerwent	Venta Silurum
4	Caister-by-Norwich	Venta Icenorum
5	Canterbury	Durnovernum Cantiacorum
6	Carlisle	Luguvalium
7	Carmarthen	Moridunum
8	Chichester	Noviomagus Reg(i)norum
9	Cirencester	Corinium Dobunnorum
10	Corbridge	Coriosopitum
11	Ilchester	Lindinis Durotrigum
12	Exeter	Isca Dumnoniorum
13	Dorchester	Durnovaria
14	Leicester	Ratae Corieltauvorum
15	Silchester	Calleva Atrebatum
16	Winchester	Venta Belgarum
17	Wroxeter	Viroconium Cornoviorum
18	Colchester	Camulodunum
19	Gloucester	Gleva, Colonia Nervia Glevensium
20	Lincoln	Lindum, Colonia Lindensium
21	London	Londinium
22	St Albans	Verulamium
23	York	Eburacum
24	Caerleon	Isca
25	Chester	Deva
26	Inchtuthil	Pinnata Castra?

Key to map of Roman Britain (opposite).

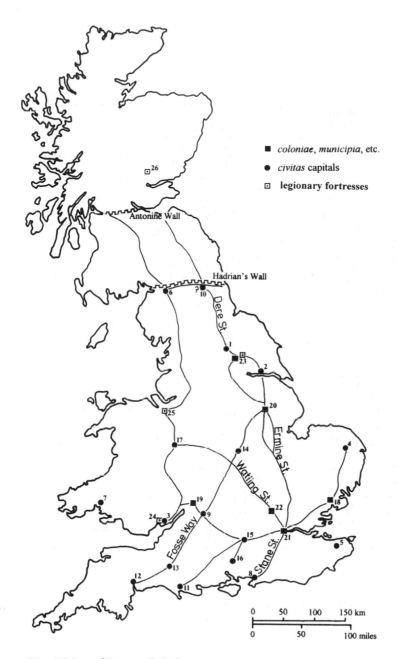

Fig. 1 Map of Roman Britain

Chapter 1
Introduction

A book like this can only serve as an introduction to a very wide subject about which much has been written. The first question to be answered, and the one which justifies having such a volume at all, is 'What is the point of studying Roman Britain?' At the simplest level the answer is surely that the subject is an intrinsically interesting one, especially if you live in Britain and are looking for a context for, even an explanation of, the monuments which are on your doorstep. But there is a deeper, more academic, answer as well. Our largest surviving written 'source' for Roman Britain, Tacitus' *Agricola*, was not intended by its author to be history as such, and other references to Britain in the surviving ancient sources tend to be passing and incidental rather than comprehensive. The historical evidence for Roman Britain is, accordingly, somewhat patchy. When, however, the historical accounts are considered alongside the complementary resource which comprises the physical remains of Roman Britain, we find that the whole record is rich and informative, and has become much more so in the last thirty years or so. One special aspect of Roman Britain as a subject is that its archaeology has been better reported, and studied in more detail, than that of most other provinces of the Roman empire.

Britain was unusual as a Roman province, especially since it was occupied late in the process of expansion of the Roman empire, and since it was remote from the core of the empire in terms both of culture and geography. Britain is also an unusual province to study since the ever-growing amount of evidence from material culture exceeds the extent of the historical record.

Britain in the Roman Empire
Before embarking on the study of 'Roman Britain' a few words of caution are necessary with regard to definitions. The terms 'Roman' and 'Britain' must first be examined in their own right, as the Roman occupation of Britain has to be seen in the broad context of Roman history in general and of the Roman empire as a whole. The island of

1

Britain and its inhabitants did not become instantly 'Roman' as the result of Caesar or Claudius crossing the English Channel, and it was not fully 'Romanised' even by the time of the building of Hadrian's Wall. This is true in spite of the fact that Roman influence was felt long before Julius Caesar and Claudius, since as a result of whatever process of trade and cultural exchange various parts of Britain, by the first century BC, had coinage, wheel-made pottery and major lowland centres of settlement. Nor was the island, or even that part of it under formal Roman control, completely Romanised by AD 410 when Honorius decided to leave the Britons to fend for themselves. The subject of this book, therefore, will be that of Britain during the period of Roman influence and domination, that is to say from the first century BC through to the early fifth century AD. The much abused term 'Romano-British' can appropriately be applied to some artefacts, such as many sculptured tombstones, which betray a fusion of Roman and native British culture, or to Romanised individuals of native stock during the long period of Roman occupation. But we must be careful to avoid applying the term indiscriminately to objects or peoples which remained purely Roman or purely British throughout the period under consideration. The same problem arises with the term 'Romanisation', since the process of increasing Roman military and political control of the province of Britannia led to a two-way exchange of ideas and culture. It must always be remembered that, just as the Britons, as a variety of tribal groupings, did not have a totally uniform cultural identity, so too the Romans, influenced by the many Mediterranean peoples with whom they had come into contact, especially the eastern and Greek societies, had a diverse and complex cultural heritage.

As a general rule, when the Romans acquired new territory they thought in terms of people and communities rather than geography. Throughout most of the Classical world this meant dealing with cities. But, by the time of the inclusion of Britain within the Roman empire, the Romans had acquired a considerable degree of experience in dealing with areas where the city was not the automatic and natural unit of society and government. Tribal rather than urban social groupings were a sign of the barbarian, and such societies stood outside the Classical core of the Roman empire in terms of language, politics, culture and physical appearance. Where no cities existed, the Romans established them as a means of political control, and inhabitants of 'uncivilised' regions (*i.e.* those areas which had no cities) rushed to embrace the material benefits which cities offered, even at the cost of abandoning sites which had been tribal centres for generations. The system of exploiting urbanisation as the driving force of Romanisation became standard under the Julio-Claudians, but even in the late Republic generals such as Pompey saw to the establishment and re-establishment of cities, which, as in the case of Pompeiopolis in Cilicia (now southern Turkey), often acquired complex names honouring their own personal names. 'Client-kings', notably those of southern Asia Minor, who ruled territories adjacent to provinces under direct Roman rule and had more or less binding treaty alliances with the Romans, often enough themselves performed the task of extending urbanisation in their own kingdoms. This was a largely unplanned process which most often served as a convenient preparatory stage before full Roman annexation. In the case of Britain under the Romans, the old tribal (*civitas*) centres were encouraged to become regional urban capitals, and, in some cases, notably Colchester (Camulodunum), the centre of the Trinovantes, the process was well under way even before the time of Claudius' invasion.

Britain's position in the empire as a whole also requires examination. Roman imperialism was not, by and large, the product of any overall grand strategy. Rather it was a haphazard process, driven, at least during the Republican period, more by the aspirations and political needs of individual generals than by any centrally recognised need for expansion for economic gain. When Julius Caesar crossed the English Channel in 55 BC he had a strong personal, and largely political, need to ensure the continuation of his military command in Gaul which was the most significant basis for the perpetuation of his political position in Rome. After two incursions Caesar left Britain as unfinished business. His move into Britain marked the end of his Gallic campaigns which had been something of a landmark in Roman history, since they represented a move away from the familiar confines of territories adjoining the Mediterranean. Like Crassus' contemporary, but disastrous, move into Parthia, Caesar's Gallic campaigns marked a new type of territorial aggrandisement that committed the Roman empire to control by long lines of land-based, rather than sea-based, communications. Acquisitions north of the Alps were more expensively gained and more expensively controlled than any previous territorial acquisitions, and Caesar's Gallic campaigns were among the first to be conducted for blatantly expansionist reasons rather than for ostensibly defensive or accidental reasons.

Caesar's settlement, if you can call it such, of Britain did not leave it as a new province. Instead he cemented treaty relationships with

British tribal leaders, who were meant to protect Roman interests against those of other more hostile British tribes. All this was fully in line with traditional policy in the Roman Republic. For what Caesar did was to create a buffer zone with friendly kings ('client-kings') who would deprive any insurgent movements which might have grown up in the new continental Gallic (i.e. Celtic) provinces of support from their cultural relatives in the not-yet-conquered island territory of Britain.

Claudius' motives for becoming involved in Britain were essentially little different from those of Caesar, though his aims were clearer and the settlement at the end of Claudius' campaigns was accordingly more definitive. Claudius also needed a great military command to maintain his political position at Rome. But there was a further incitement to Claudius to invade Britain, which had developed after the period of relatively passive attitudes to relations with Britain under Augustus and Tiberius. Those emperors had kept their distance from the island, but Gaius Caligula (reigned AD 37-41) had begun to show a renewed interest in extending the Roman empire across the channel. Claudius thus inherited a situation in which the armies massed in Gaul and Germany were eating the agricultural production of those provinces, whilst they waited poised for the invasion of Britain. And Claudius was a demonstrably weak emperor who needed a striking military success to secure his own political position as ruler of the Roman world. In other words the Roman action in occupying Britain must be seen as motivated by considerations beyond simple imperialism and territorial aggrandisement, and certainly not as part of some coherently thought through imperial strategy.

All this is not to say that the Roman empire derived no profit from the addition to it of the new province of Britannia. Exploitation of territory tended to follow acquisition and was not necessarily the primary reason for that acquisition. Any newly acquired province in the Roman empire was a source of financial revenue through taxation and exploitation of natural resources. Yet new provinces also required maintenance and the provision of standing armies for a considerable time after the initial period of conquest. In the case of Britain, unlike some of the Mediterranean provinces, the Roman military force was never removed throughout its history as a province. This is because the island was never completely occupied, so that the presence of the army was necessary to protect the provincials (the 'Romano-British', if you like) who lived within the bounds of Roman authority from those natives who lived 'beyond the pale'. For Claudius the removal of armies from Germany to Britain may well have ended an inherited unproductive drain on resources. But for the inhabitants of Romano-British cities like Verulamium (St. Albans), after the shock of undergoing conquest and Roman domination had abated, the presence of the Roman army to the north of them would have been a beneficial aspect of their subjugation.

One of the most interesting aspects of the Roman occupation of the island of Britain is that it was never completed. Instead, by the early part of the second century AD, a clear policy of drawing a line across northern Britain had been established. The line moved from Hadrian's line to Antoninus Pius' and back again, but a significant part of the British isles, including most of Scotland and the whole of Ireland, was never brought into Roman possession. The kind of thinking which is represented by the frontiers of northern Britain would have been unimaginable at the time of Julius Caesar, and the first century of Roman occupation of Britain is thus of considerable interest for the light it sheds on the broad shift of Roman imperial thinking from bold expansionism to fixed territorialism. Nowhere else in the Roman empire is this shift so clearly demonstrated.

6

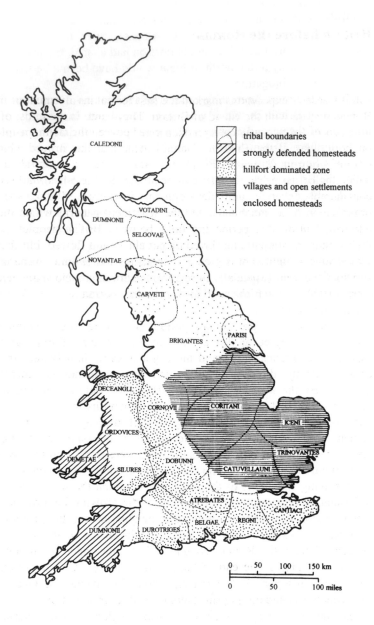

Fig. 2 Relation of the *civitates* to settlement types (after Millett 1990).

Chapter 2
Britain before the Romans

Julius Caesar's expeditions marked the first formal involvement of the Roman empire with the island of Britain. They came in the midst of a long process of two-way cultural exchange between the Celtic peoples on both sides of the English Channel. Although the Britain which Caesar confronted was still in the Iron Age in cultural and technological terms, in the last two centuries BC the island had seen considerable change and development in terms of the social organisation of its inhabitants and the settlement patterns which they adopted. During this period the links between British peoples and their Celtic counterparts on the continent ebbed and flowed, but there was always a significant degree of interaction and cultural exchange, and some patterns (especially in relation to agriculture and settlement) were established which continued into the period of the Roman occupation of Britain.

Throughout the pre-Roman period, too, there was continuing trade. As the degree of Roman influence in northern Europe grew, especially in France, more and more goods came into Britain from areas within the direct orbit of Roman and continental commercial interests. By the late second century BC Gallo-Belgic gold coinage had arrived in Britain and Italian wine had found its way to the south coast of the island and, presumably through trading centres like the settlement at Hengistbury Head, to the tables of some British tribal leaders. The quantities of imports involved were small, and they were of minimal significance within the British economy as a whole. Yet the surviving fragments of the amphorae in which the wine travelled to Britain serve as a physical reminder of the growing importance of Rome to Iron Age Britain's immediate neighbours and the proximity of Britain to Rome's growing sphere of influence in the last two centuries before the Roman conquest. The appearance of imported goods in Britain at the end of the second century BC is significant since that was a period of increasing Roman involvement in Gaul, an area which was undergoing substantial social re-organisation.

Britain, as seen by Caesar, was a tribal region, split into various entities, but showing emerging signs of organisation and cohesion, at least in the case of the peoples occupying south-eastern England, an area which was still the destination of tribal units emigrating from the continent. It has often been proposed that pre-Roman Iron age Britain can be seen as a set of culturally distinct zones reflecting different waves of incoming peoples arriving from continental Europe from about the seventh century BC onwards. This idea is probably too simplistic. Yet consideration of the different types of settlement in Britain by the first century AD (Fig. 2) suggests that the western and northern zones of Britain were less culturally sophisticated than the southeastern areas which Caesar knew. The level of cohesion shown by the British tribes under the leadership of Cunobelinus is itself an indicator of the degree of social development in the late pre-Roman period. In much of Britain the dominant settlement pattern was one of small, defended sites, basically separate and independent agricultural units, whose people perhaps came together under the leadership of local chieftains during times of duress. But Cunobelinus led an alliance of important tribes from Camulodunum, a large, nucleated lowland settlement with extensive defences, which, however irregular and disconnected, were impressive enough. Camulodunum was not a city in the full constitutional sense implied by the Latin word *urbs*, though, as a native town, it merited the title of *oppidum*. It was much closer to the Classical urban concept than the massively defended hillforts of south-west England such as Maiden Castle and Hod Hill in Dorset.

The impact of greater Roman interest in Britain in the pre-Conquest period can nevertheless be detected by looking at the hillforts of the late pre-Roman Iron Age. Large hillforts like Maiden Castle and Hod Hill had been emerging as territorial capitals during the third and second centuries BC. But there had also been signs of a population shift from upland sites to extensive lowland settlements, the *oppida*, such as Bagendon (by Cirencester), Colchester (Camulodunum), Prae Wood (by St. Albans), and Silchester (Calleva). These centres of population had street systems and were a focus for industrial activity and even coin production. They were protected by massive linear dykes and earthen banks, though these were irregularly planned and often discontinuous. The *oppida* often occupied greater areas than the hillforts. But there was a move to re-fortify the hillfort sites at about the time of Caesar's incursions, and in the west and north of Britain the hillforts in any case remained in use until the Roman occupation. Their significance as centres of native culture and potential resistance is amply demonstrated by the fact that they were often levelled after being taken by Roman arms. Thus the inhabitants of Maiden Castle were moved to the lowland city site of Dorchester (Durnovaria), and Wroxeter (Viroconium) was established on low land near the Wrekin in Shropshire. Meanwhile, for a short period, a Roman fort was created within the great hillfort at Hod Hill. Even oppida could be re-established in a similar manner, since Corinium (Cirencester) was created in the river valley below the site of Bagendon. The reasons behind these shifts in the location of centres of population were doubtless military and political in the first instance, and the new sites, which had direct access to the road system, combined the advantages of being much more easily controlled at the same time as being in a better position from the commercial point of view.

Economy
The economy of pre-Roman Britain was predominantly agricultural, and it remained so after the Roman conquest. Although the Romans brought with them new crops as well as improved technology, involving increased use of iron for tools and machinery, the effect of Roman changes was to improve productivity rather than bringing about a major agricultural revolution. Thus a trend towards more intensive and efficient farming practices, which had been developing before the Roman conquest, was moved further forward. This was bound to have consequences in the sense that a stronger agricultural economy could support a higher population. The new technology, or rather greater availability of iron products, meant that clearance of traditional forest areas was more easily accomplished and the heavy clay soils, especially in the Midlands, could more easily be ploughed. The traditional pattern of Iron Age Britain was one of mixed farming with even the more mountainous parts of Wales and northern England having substantial arable pockets in what were predominantly pastoral zones. But in the period immediately before the Roman occupation and during the early centuries of that occupation, there was an increase in the amount of land which could be brought into arable production. This in turn created the need and resource for an intensification of urban settlement. The processes of urban foundation which were driven by military and political considerations immediately after the conquest were subsequently continued as a result of economic development. The new circumstances must have been confusing for a native population which was used to more diffuse patterns of social organisation. Yet the early provincial revolt

under Boudicca was prompted at least in part by reaction to excessive Roman milking of the new benefits of provincial organisation.

Whilst the economy of immediately pre-Roman Britain was strengthening, and agricultural production increasing, it is important to remember that the country saw very irregular patterns of social organisation. This is reflected in the material remains which indicate that, in the late pre-Roman Iron Age, much of Britain was still without wheel-made pottery and coins. Moreover, the differentiation in social and settlement terms were as much determined by varying arable and pastoral farming systems as by the process of waves of cultural invasion. The main distinction between hillforts and small, individual farmsteads, with the alternative social grouping systems which these different types of settlements imply, reflect in substantial part the distinction between arable and pastoral groupings. Although variation in settlement type was also, of course, determined by geography and geology, a number of factors ensured that social patterns were most centralised and hierarchical in southern and eastern Britain, where the range of settlement size from farmstead to hillfort is most extreme. By contrast, in western and northern Britain settlements were more uniform in size, with the majority of sites being defended farmsteads. The Romans first came into contact, therefore, with that part of Britain where social patterns came nearest to those they would have recognised. The subsequent decision not to conquer northern Britain was presumably basically an economic one, but it is likely that even the 'Britons' of central and southern England would have regarded the inhabitants of the lands beyond Hadrian's Wall as too primitive and 'barbarian' to be brought into civilised (i.e. urbanised) social order.

The People of Iron Age Britain
What were the people themselves like? It is ironic that the appearance of the Britons and the ways in which British society was organised have to be reconstructed by a combination of reasoning forward from the material remains and from accounts in the Classical writers. In general terms the picture which emerges from the ancient literary sources confirms the pattern which can be detected from the archaeological record. Julius Caesar, whose experience, of course, was predominantly related to southeastern Britain, offers the following description:

> 12.   The interior of Britain is inhabited by people who claim
> on the strength of their own tradition to be indigenous to the
> island; the coastal districts by immigrants from Belgic territory

who came after plunder and to make war - nearly all of them called after the tribes from which they originated. Following their invasion they settled down there and began to till the fields. The population is very large, their homesteads thick on the ground and very much like those in Gaul, and the cattle numerous. As money they use either bronze or gold coins or iron bars with a fixed standard of weight.... There is every type of timber as in Gaul, with the exception of beech and pine. They have a taboo against eating hare, chicken, and goose, but they rear them for amusement and pleasure. The climate is more temperate than in Gaul, the cold spells being less severe.

14. Of all the Britons by far the most civilised are the inhabitants of Cantium (Kent), a purely maritime region, whose way of life is little different from that of the Gauls. Most of those inhabiting the interior do not grow corn, but live instead on milk and wheat and clothe themselves in skins. All the Britons dye themselves with woad, which produces a blue colour, and as a result their appearance in battle is all the more daunting. They wear their hair long, and shave all their bodies with the exception of their heads and upper lip. Wives are shared between groups of ten or twelve men, especially between brothers and between fathers and sons. The offspring on the other hand are considered the children of the man with whom the women first lived.

(CAESAR, *Gallic War* V 12 and 14)

Strabo, who wrote towards the end of the 1st century BC, during the reign of Augustus, added the following information:

The men (of Britain) are taller than the Gauls, not so blond, and of looser build. As an indication of their size I myself saw some in Rome little more than boys standing as much as half a foot above the tallest in the city, though they were bow-legged and in some respects lacking any gracefulness of body. Their customs are in some respects like those of the Gauls, in other respects simpler and more barbaric. As a result, some of them, through their want of skill, do not make cheese, though they have no shortage of milk. They are also unskilled in horticulture or farming in general. They are ruled by chieftains. In war they mostly use chariots like some of the Gauls. The forests are their cities, for they fortify a large circular enclosure

with felled trees and there make themselves huts and pen their
cattle, though not for a long stay.

(STRABO, *Geography* IV 5,2)

The evidence from Caesar's accounts of his campaigns in Britain casts
useful light on the social order of British society, since he is clearly
dealing with a complex tribal system in which relatively small units
came together at time of stress. Each of these units seems to have its
own chieftain and aristocratic élite, and Cassivellaunus was leader of a
somewhat ragged grouping of these units. Caesar's accounts of Britain
also indicate the presence of a priestly class, and warriors among the
aristocratic élite, with the lower social order being attached to the élite
group by systems of clientage. The pattern is directly comparable with
the picture of social organisation in Gaul which emerges from the
main part of Caesar's account of his Gallic wars. At the end of
Caesar's campaign in Britain five groups seem to have broken from
Cassivellaunus' leadership in order to surrender to Caesar. Doubtless
the same social systems were operating when Claudius invaded,
though the literary evidence for this is lacking. Caesar's account must
be treated with due regard to the fact that he described a situation
when the British tribes were united against an external threat. There
may have been more internal bickering and disunity when that threat
was not present.

The precise distribution of the tribes is not completely understood,
but the main tribal areas are well defined (Fig. 2). The tribal areas can
be detected from the artefactual evidence, notably from consideration
of the distribution of coinage, from evidence from the cemeteries, and
from stylistic considerations like the different types of decoration
which appear on late Iron Age pottery. After Caesar's departure from
Britain the Roman empire was convulsed by a series of civil wars, and
Britain was essentially left alone. It is interesting, therefore, to note
that these tribal arrangements in Britain were shifting in the period
between Caesar and Claudius. This was probably a normal state of
affairs, and one effect of the Roman occupation was, in effect, to
fossilise the tribal zones as they were at the point of Claudius'
conquest.

Chapter 3
Historical Outline

Sources

The historical record of Roman Britain, like that for most of antiquity, is patchy. What we know is derived from a combination of literary documents and the archaeological record, be this in the form of inscriptions and coins designed to mark a particular event, or the sites established by the Romans and the artefacts they produced. What unites them as sources is the accident of survival. The chance survival of one document or inscription, for instance, or the loss of another means that some periods seem overcrowded with detail while others are marked by a tantalising vagueness, with apparently important events merely glimpsed against a background of uncertainty or represented by archaeological remains that pose more questions than they provide answers. The result is a real danger of disproportionate importance being attached to those periods where the historical record is rich. Then too the sources themselves can be misleading. This is particularly so with our two most detailed literary records, Caesar's *Gallic War* and Tacitus' *Agricola*. The first, for all its aura of objectivity, remains autobiographical, and it is clear that Caesar has often slanted his narrative for propaganda purposes. The second is more overtly partisan, a quasi-biography written by Agricola's son-in-law, and designed to elevate the man above his predecessors as governor of Britain. Both, though, share the merit of being closely linked in time with the events described. This is not the case, however, with all such sources. Many are widely separated from the events they describe in terms of time, and are often reliant on earlier works, the objectivity of which is wholly unknown. So the student of Roman Britain's historical record must be constantly aware of the potential traps along the way and be ever ready to question the validity of what he or she finds. For obvious reasons the scope of the present section precludes a full narrative account of the four centuries of Roman occupation. Instead it seeks to point out the major developments, to indicate the major sources available, in particular the literary record, and to pose questions of their contents.

Caesar's First Invasion 55 BC (Gallic War IV 20-38)
Causes: Caesar mentions only two factors that led to his first invasion of Britain: (1) British involvement in resistance to his conquest of Gaul; (2) the advantage to be gained from a reconnaissance of the island. In military terms neither makes much sense. The first seems directed more towards circumventing the law that forbade governors from going beyond their provinces except to counter external interference and neutralising those in Rome who were claiming that Gaul was by now fully pacified and no longer needed Caesar's presence - a clear attempt to denude him of his power-base, the troops at his disposal. What Caesar was relying on was not the reality of any threat Britain posed to the Roman position in Gaul, but rather the perception of it. The claim, like the idea of Britain providing a safe haven for Gallic dissidents, could be guaranteed to provoke an automatic response in Roman minds that Caesar could manipulate for his own purposes. The second factor is an even less valid reason for invasion, yet provides a clue to the truth in the word 'advantage'. In military terms there was nothing to be gained from an expedition to Britain at the very end of the campaigning season in 55 BC, with scant preparation, virtually no advance knowledge of what conditions would be encountered, and little in the way of supplies. If anything, such a campaign would be strategically inept. Caesar must have expected his rivals, Pompey and Crassus, to cover themselves with glory once they had ceased to be consuls in Rome and had moved to their proconsular provinces in 54. A pre-emptive bid for attention in 55, therefore, by a push into what for Roman eyes was a land beyond the known world, was not only 'more important than the conquest of petty (Gallic) tribes' (*GW* IV 22), it was essential. Such a venture of course speaks volumes about Caesar's ultimate priorities, in that both Britain and his own army were mere pawns in a wider political power struggle.

Events: Close reading of Caesar's account shows the whole expedition was from start to finish a potential shambles held together by skilful adaptation and reaction to events, and by sheer luck. Despite attempts to gain some knowledge of the terrain into which he was moving through reconnaissance by Volusenus and the questioning of native traders, Caesar was clearly heading into the unknown. His aim was a show of force at minimal cost: hence the eager welcome given to envoys from the tribes of SE Britain who had learned of Caesar's plans and were themselves anxious to minimise losses. This explains in turn the despatch of Caesar's Gallic agent, Commius of the Atrebates, whose instructions were to foster such amenable attitudes elsewhere in Britain. In the event, however, Commius was arrested the moment he stepped ashore. Yet the apparent run of success that ostensibly marked Caesar's preparations disguised an inherently unstable situation. Caesar's entry into Britain was made with only two legions, the VII & X, and in boats that were largely a prey to wind and tide, a factor which largely removed much of his choice of landing place. Their construction too was unsuitable for beaching in shallow water and Caesar had seriously misread the reality behind British overtures. Only the use of more manoeuvrable warships and the bravado of the X Legion's standard-bearer staved off a beachhead disaster at the hands of the British 'welcoming committee'. Thereafter the campaign was a cat-and-mouse game, with the Britons offering co-operation (such as the release of Commius) when Caesar looked strong, but turning hostile when things went badly for him - as they soon did. And without cavalry Caesar had no answer to the British war-chariot, a weapon he had never experienced on the continent and which gave the Britons speed and stability in attack. The Roman cavalry that should have come never arrived, driven back in its second attempted crossing by a storm that also wrecked many of Caesar's troop transports, virtually marooning him in Britain with few supplies and with the end of the sailing season imminent. The Britons were aware that time was on their side, and their attack on the VII legion foraging in the fields might have seen the end of Rome's incursion. But Caesar's luck once again held, allowing him to rescue the beleaguered legion and to counter the chariots with a band of cavalry that Commius had attracted to himself. This in turn provided the stalemate Caesar could exploit to cover his withdrawal from Britain and to claim the paper victory he needed. Militarily, the campaign was a near disaster, but in its perception by Rome it proved a great propaganda ploy, as shown by the award of a public thanksgiving 20 days long, an unprecedented period and five days longer than that given for the more tangible conquest of Gaul. Such was the awe that crossing the Channel inspired.

Caesar's Second Invasion 54 BC (Gallic War V 1-23)
Caesar nowhere states explicitly the reason for the second invasion. Was he hoping to exploit the popular favour that had greeted the 55 expedition with more realistic gains? Does the presence of private vessels in the armada point to the hope for commerce or booty, the

latter being something Caesar's own depleted resources desperately needed? Was there an element of injured pride at not achieving true military success the previous year? The scale of the invasion, certainly, shows altered priorities: five legions out of the eight at his disposal instead of two, more warships for inshore work, transports designed with a shallower draught and fitted with oars for manoeuvrability, and 2000 cavalry. The very size of the fleet involved - a total of 800 ships - in fact had an unforeseen advantage in deterring any British resistance on the shore. From his beachhead Caesar's plan for a lightning strike inland before the Britons could mass in strength was a tactic that had worked well on the continent, and worked in Britain for 24 hours. But in choosing the same area in which to make his landfall as in 55 Caesar had made his first mistake. While his forces were taking the first British stronghold they came upon - probably Bigbury - a storm was wreaking havoc among the fleet. The withdrawal to the beachhead that this necessitated and the ten days taken in dragging his ships completely out of the water lost Caesar the initiative and allowed the Britons both to regroup under the unified command of Cassivellaunus, and to present a far more formidable obstacle when the advance was resumed. Once again there was the same British probing for Roman weaknesses. Exploiting the advantage given by their chariots they attacked Roman forces as they fortified their marching camp, and then made a speedy getaway when Caesar threw in extra units to rescue troops who were clearly disconcerted by enemy tactics. Mistakes, however, were not confined to the Roman side. The attempt to repeat the events of 55 with an attack on foragers came badly unstuck when the Britons found themselves faced not by one legion but by three and the whole force of cavalry. The resulting British defeat was, in fact, one of the turning points of the whole campaign: (1) It caused the alliance that had gathered around Cassivellaunus to wither; and (2) it opened up the crossing of the Thames and with it penetration of Cassivellaunus' own territory. Yet in the give-and-take of war the British leader was not yet beaten. By removing anything of use from the line of Caesar's advance and using his chariots to prevent the Romans advancing on a wide front, he clearly aimed to minimise damage to his own territory and to draw out the enemy's lines of communications until they could be severed. At this point, however, the second turning point of the campaign occurred when Cassivellaunus' earlier aggression against the Trinovantes of Essex caused them to take the Roman side. In return for the restoration of their prince, Mandubracius, whose father had been killed by Cassivellaunus, they offered those two items that Caesar must have been desperate for: supplies and information, in particular information concerning the whereabouts of Cassivellaunus' main stronghold. Fair treatment of the Trinovantes brought overtures from other tribes, and the capture of the stronghold cost Cassivellaunus much of his power-base. When his final ploy - an attack on the Roman base-camp by the four kings who ruled in Kent - also failed, the only course open was to sue for peace. The situation was not all one-sided, however, since Caesar's early loss of the initiative had deprived him of that easy and quick victory he no doubt wanted. Winter was now approaching and the signs coming from Gaul were not good. They were enough in fact to have convinced Caesar already that his early return to the continent was essential. Besides, to leave a garrison behind in a Britain far from pacified would be folly. Thus, after fixing an annual tribute and receiving assurances that Mandubracius would not be harmed, Caesar withdrew once again to Gaul.

In military terms the 54 invasion was decidedly more successful than that in 55, but in other respects it brought few gains; hence perhaps Caesar's silence as to his actual aims. Caesar likewise gives no hint of the popular reaction in Rome, which in itself suggests there was nothing like the earlier enthusiasm, and letters from the politician Cicero are heavy with ironic depreciation. In economic terms too the expedition seems to have fallen far short of expectations.

Caesar to Claudius

With any thoughts Caesar may have had for a third expedition cut short by events leading to the great Gallic uprising of Vercingetorix and then the civil war against Pompey, relations between Rome and Britain settled into an effective state of mutual non-interference. From the Roman side the upsurge in trade that followed on from Caesar's contacts was reckoned to bring in more revenue than any conquest could (Strabo II 5,8, V 5,3). For many British tribes Rome was seen as a welcome counterbalance to threats of territorial expansion by more immediate neighbours, as Caesar's successor, the Emperor Augustus, was to demonstrate by a succession of threatened invasions - all ostensibly cancelled only because of more pressing needs elsewhere. Likewise it was to Rome that rulers displaced by internal coups d'état or external pressure fled for refuge. We hear for instance of a Dubnovellaunus and of Tincommius, son of the Commius who had assisted Caesar in 55 but who subsequently changed sides during the

Gallic uprising and was forced to escape to Britain. Under Augustus' own successor, Tiberius, there was even less Roman interest in the fluctuations of internal British politics, fluctuations for which the main source of evidence lies in the coinage produced. The accession of the idiosyncratic Gaius Caligula in AD 37, however, was to herald a radical shift in Roman policy. Inspired by the arrival at the imperial court of the exiled prince Adminius, a son of the Catuvellaunian king Cunobelinus, Caligula embarked upon an attempted invasion in 40, universally condemned by our ancient sources (Suetonius *Caligula* 44-6, Dio LIX 25). The narrative, though, contains more than a hint that the infamous order - for the Roman forces poised on the coast of Gaul to gather sea-shells - was not so much a sign of madness as Caligula's reaction to his troops' refusal to venture into territory still viewed with awe.

The Claudian Invasion (Dio LX 19-24, Suetonius Claudius 17)
Causes: Like Caesar's expedition in 55 BC the invasion launched by the Emperor Claudius in AD 43 sprang from a convergence of public and private interests. In terms of public policy, the escalation of tribal instability in Britain - the expulsion of Verica, king of the Atrebates, and British demands for his extradition - was chosen to be viewed in Rome as a challenge to the empire's power and authority. In personal terms, Claudius clearly saw in Britain the possibility of acquiring that military glory on which his very existence relied. For much of his life Claudius had lived surrounded by relatives who had won popular acclaim through military victories; yet because of physical infirmities he himself had been forced to live in seclusion or worse, derision, the fool of the imperial family. On the assassination of Caligula in AD 41 he had been elevated by the Praetorian Guard, almost as a whim. Unless he proved himself in military terms, what support he enjoyed could evaporate just as quickly. This he had to avoid, and what better way than to outdo the great Julius Caesar himself? After the wild extravagance of Caligula there was also a pressing need to replenish the imperial treasury, and war booty that Britain might supply was a tempting prospect. More importantly, Caligula's creation of additional legions, now stationed on the NW frontier, was both a drain on resources and created a military imbalance in the empire that an unscrupulous commander might exploit to advance his own imperial aspirations. To employ them in garrisoning Britain on the other hand would immediately solve the problems their very existence created.

Events: Since Claudius could not afford to fail he went for overkill in terms of the forces deployed against Britain: four legions and an equal number of auxiliary troops, in all a total of 40,000 men under the command of Aulus Plautius. As in Caligula's day, the troops were reluctant to embark and the attempt by one of Claudius' ministers, the freedman Narcissus, to instruct them in their duty might have proved fatal to the expedition had not Roman humour at the thought of an ex-slave lecturing free men intervened. The incident, though, had one unexpected result in that the delay aroused in British minds expectations of another Caligulan fiasco. As a result, they failed to oppose the Roman landing and thus lost any hope of gaining the initiative. Dio's narrative of the expedition reports that the crossing was made 'in three divisions so as not to be hindered in landing'. One of these landing places was undoubtedly Richborough, which was to remain the official port of entry into Britain thereafter, but dispute surrounds the whereabouts or even the existence of the other two. When native resistance was eventually encountered, it was led, as in 54 BC, by the Catuvellauni under Caratacus and Togodumnus, sons of the now dead Cunobelinus. As in 54, smouldering resentment at Catuvellaunian imperialism in the past combined with recognition of Rome's military might to produce defections from the British alliance at the first signs of reverse. Yet this is balanced by Dio's report of stiffening British resistance in response to Togodumnus' death, which came after Roman victories at the Medway and Thames. But was Plautius' decision to halt the advance at this point really caused by fear, as Dio's account suggests, or did the resistance merely provide him with the pretext for holding on to his gains while he sent for the emperor, who wanted to be present at the final victory? When Claudius arrived, he brought with him additional forces and elephants, which doubtless lent an exotic air to his triumphant entry into the enemy capital, Colchester (Camulodunum). There he received the surrender of British tribes and left the newly created province after a stay of only 16 days.

Provincial Expansion (Suetonius Vespasian 4, Tacitus Annals XII 31-9)

Following the initial conquest, the next task was clearly consolidation of those areas already gained and expansion into regions which had either surrendered voluntarily or which offered some strategic gain. To this end the legions fanned out from their concentration in Colchester. While the XX Valeria legion remained in the new provincial capital in order to hold the SE, the IX Hispana headed north towards the Humber, the XIV Gemina NW over the Midlands and the II Augusta, under the command of the future Emperor Vespasian, into the west country, where the claim that he reduced numerous hill-forts is fully borne out by the discovery of Roman ballista bolts inside native defensive positions such as Maiden Castle in Dorset. Likewise, the effectiveness of such artillery against forces armed with nothing more powerful than the arrow or sling is amply demonstrated by discovery of a skeleton with a bolt still embedded in its spine.

In 47, after the normal three year period in office Plautius was replaced by Ostorius Scapula. For their part the natives took advantage of the new arrival's unfamiliarity with the country to engage in raiding parties. In reply Ostorius sought further consolidation by disarming all tribes under Roman control. As a tactical move it made sense, but in political terms it displayed an ineptitude and refusal to consider the susceptibilities of provincials for which Rome was to pay dearly over the years. As part of the initial settlement Rome had looked with particular favour on some tribes whose leaders had voluntarily entered into treaty relations - the so-called client states - allowing them to maintain their native forms of government and the right to bear arms. In return such clients freed Roman forces for more effective use in frontier districts. The two most famous tribes in this category were the Regni under Cogidubnus, who never wavered in his loyalty to Rome, and the Iceni of Norfolk, who reacted to Scapula's policy with revolt, sparking off perhaps that resentment later to flare up again into the Boudiccan rebellion. With not a little trouble the uprising was crushed and Scapula then determined upon an advance into north Wales, ostensibly designed to drive a wedge between unconquered regions to the north and the west of the province. However, an unfavourable reaction to this on the part of the Brigantes in the north - and thus the prospect of simultaneous trouble on two fronts - was enough to convince Scapula of the wisdom of a tactical withdrawal. In S Wales the Silures were themselves proving a major problem under the leadership of Caratacus, who may have lost his native home-base among the Catuvellauni but had now found another. It was only, in fact, by moving the XX Valeria from Colchester, which now became a colony (*colonia*, see Ch. 5), to a new fortress at Gloucester (Gleva) that they were held in check. At this point indeed Caratacus seems to have become the main target of Roman attention. Military offensives in S

Wales forced him to move his sphere of operations first to the territory of the Ordovices in N Wales and from there, after defeat and the capture of his family, to Brigantia under its queen Cartimandua. Doubtless Caratacus aimed to establish here yet another base for continued resistance; Cartimandua on the other hand was determined not to see her own position usurped or her tribe's freedom from Roman interference disturbed. As a result Caratacus was arrested and handed over to Scapula in 51. Surprisingly, Caratacus did not meet the usual fate of foreign leaders, an ignominious execution, but was allowed by Claudius an honourable retirement. Despite the loss of such a figure, however, conditions in Britain showed no signs of settling, with further serious unrest among the Silures, who were alarmed by reports of Scapula's intention to wipe them out - yet another instance of Roman disdain for native populations. The truth of the reports we cannot gauge, but the tribe was saved from its fate by the death of Scapula while still in office. His successor, Didius Gallus, was soon faced by yet more problems, first from the Silures, then the Brigantes. Cartimandua's treatment of Caratacus had in fact split the tribe, with the anti-Roman faction led by the queen's own husband, Venutius. However, so long as the Romans were able to intervene on the queen's side, Venutius was obliged to bide his time.

Didius' term in office ended in 57 and it was operations once more against the Silures that occupied his successor, Quintus Veranius, until his own death in 58. Into his place now came Suetonius Paulinus, whose career in Britain in many ways mirrored that of Scapula, with a move into N Wales (including an invasion of Anglesey and the only reported confrontation between Roman and Druid in Britain), followed by a second and more bloody revolt on the part of the Iceni.

The Boudiccan Rebellion (Tacitus Annals XIV 29-37, Dio LXII 1-12)
Causes: On the death of Prasutagus, king of the Iceni, the Roman decision to incorporate the kingdom fully into the structure of the province brought protests from the natives and a Roman response of such gross insensitivity as to set the whole of East Anglia ablaze. Prasutagus may have foreseen the end of local autonomy as a result of his death and attempted to spare his family and tribe the worst of Roman depredations by making the Emperor Nero joint heir to his kingdom, along with his daughters. Such a course was in fact a common device to ensure the successful implementation of a will. The terms of a native will, however, seem to have made little impression on the officials sent to take over the territory. The king's widow,

Boudicca, was flogged, his daughters raped, and the local nobility driven from their ancestral estates. Yet it was upon such high-ranking natives that the Romans had relied to maintain the peace of the tribe as a whole. Nor did the ensuing revolt restrict itself to the Iceni. Among other tribes who rose were the Trinovantes of Essex who had their own grievances. Following the invasion, their capital, Colchester (Camulodunum), had become the site first of a legionary fortress, and then in 49 of a colony of veteran Roman soldiers retired from active service. But these men were not content with the grants of land around the city that were given to them; instead, they went out of their way to steal more from the natives. Worse still, the temple of the deified Claudius established in the city formed the visible sign of their subjection. To pay for it - and for many of the trappings of Roman life and culture the local nobility were expected to adopt - huge debts had been incurred and, if we accept the evidence of Dio, the recall of these (and of grants the Britons thought were outright gifts from Claudius) was a major cause of unrest. Without doubt the seeds of rebellion had long been sown by the Romans. But it was the unfortunate coincidence of Prasutagus' death and the absence of the governor in Wales that ostensibly seems to have provided the initial spark for the uprising and allowed it to grow with the disastrous speed and ferocity that were its chief characteristics.

Events: It is a measure of the extreme hatred Rome had engendered that in the ensuing events Colchester, London and St. Albans all fell in turn to Boudicca's forces with a loss, according to Tacitus, of some 70,000 Romans and native supporters. For the Roman garrison as a whole the situation was potentially dangerous, not because of any inferior fighting ability, for all that the legions were heavily outnumbered by the enemy, but because of their dispersal. The defeat of part of the IX Hispana, under its commander Petillius Cerialis, when it attempted to rescue the situation demonstrated the need for careful planning before engaging in battle. This explains (1) Paulinus' decision to abandon what he could not defend when, after the fall of Colchester, he arrived with his cavalry first in London and then in St. Albans; and (2) the need to rejoin his main force of infantry, the XIV Gemina and part of the XX Valeria, still en route from Wales. To make matters worse for Paulinus, the mauling given to the IX Hispana was compounded by the refusal of the Camp Prefect temporarily in charge of the II Augusta to move his forces from the west country. There was also a growing shortage of supplies available to the Roman troops, who had travelled light in order to travel quickly. Paulinus, therefore, needed a speedy but certain victory. To minimise his numerical inferiority he chose a site for battle where he would have the enemy only to his front. By the time of the actual engagement, somewhere in the Midlands, the combination of native over-confidence and Roman discipline brought a complete turn-around and left, if we believe Tacitus, some 80,000 British dead for a loss of only 400 Romans.

British defeat and the death of Boudicca, either through illness or suicide, was immediately followed by Roman retribution and by famine among the native population, since in their eagerness to push ahead with the revolt they had neglected their fields in the belief that they could live on looted stores. This, combined with Paulinus' determination to exact full retribution, threatened in fact to perpetuate a political and economic disaster in Britain. It was only the arrival of a new Procurator, Julius Classicianus, whose chief function was the development of Britain's economy, that brought hope for the future. Tacitus chooses to portray the clash of interests between Procurator and Governor which inevitably ensued in terms of personal animosity. More likely it arose from the opposition of their aims - Suetonius bent on vengeance, Classicianus with his Gallic background more attuned to native thinking and the needs of the province. An investigation by the imperial freedman Polyclitus, sent from Rome, papered over the dissension between the two men, but sense eventually prevailed with the replacement of Paulinus first by Petronius Turpilianus, then by Trebellius Maximus. Between them these two allowed the process of recovery to develop, even to the extent that the XIV Gemina legion was withdrawn from the province in the mid 60s, its position at Wroxeter being filled by the XX Valeria, who till then had held the S Wales frontier. In turn the XX was replaced by the II Augusta, brought up from the west country to a new legionary base at Gloucester. The Boudiccan rebellion was the last major native-led uprising Britain was to feel. The provincials for their part no doubt learned to their cost the futility of revolt. Whether the Romans learned that native sensibilities could not be totally ignored is another matter.

In the imperial upheaval that followed the forced suicide of Nero in AD 68 Britain took relatively little part. Though partisan feeling for this or that contender for imperial honours existed, and eventually forced Trebellius from the province altogether, his replacement, Vettius Bolanus, remained purposefully on the sidelines and avoided major involvement in the continental power-struggles. Only a resurgence of the quarrel between Cartimandua and Venutius, who seized the opportunity caused by Roman distractions, marred Bolanus' period of office. Despite Roman intervention the queen was driven from Brigantia and the north became an overtly hostile region that marked it out for a speedy response.

The Push North (Tacitus Agricola): Fig. 8
Because of our imperfect source record details of the action taken by Petillius Cerialis, who arrived to replace Bolanus in AD 71, are poorly documented. The fact, however, that he had served as commander of the IX Hispana during the Boudiccan rebellion and thus had intricate knowledge of the province suggests that his experience was meant to count. With him came a new legion, the II Adiutrix, to replace the XIV Gemina, which had been restored to Britain temporarily during the period 68-9. With the II Adiutrix stationed in Lincoln, the IX Hispana was moved up to York and Brigantia overrun if not actually annexed. Following subsequent moves against the Silures and central Wales by Paulinus' successor, Julius Frontinus, who pushed forward the legionary base from Gloucester to Caerleon, the stage was set for further major expansion on the arrival of Julius Agricola in 77. Like Cerialis he had already seen service in Britain - as a junior officer during the Boudiccan rebellion, and then as commander of the XX Valeria in the early 70s. A major difficulty, however, surrounds the position Agricola holds in Romano-British history. Although he undoubtedly filled the post of governor for an unprecedented period - twice the norm - the survival of a biography written by his son-in-law, Tacitus, means not only that the events of his period in office are better documented than those of any other official in the whole of the province's history, but also that his achievements are exalted far beyond what a more dispassionate account might allow. Tacitus' narrative, for instance, (1) belittles the achievements of previous governors, though it is upon their foundations that Agricola's own successes were built; (2) claims as unique achievements for Agricola in terms of civil and administrative advances what were undoubtedly part of every governor's remit; and (3) both defends what were clearly defects in Agricola's own policies in Britain and decries what in the end turned out to be more rational positions put forward by others.

The scope of the present work prevents a detailed narration of Agricola's period in office. The main events given by Tacitus, though, may be schematised as follows. (The traditional dates attached to

Agricola's career, which place events one year later than in the present volume, have been revised in recent years as a result of coin analysis.)

AD 77: Arrival in Britain. Rather than follow advice and take time to settle into his post Agricola immediately ordered the near extermination of the Ordovices in N Wales. He then proceeded to the reconquest of Anglesey. In this he was virtually repeating the earlier campaign of Paulinus and completing the reduction of Wales substantially effected in the south by Frontinus. At the same time the process of moving the II Adiutrix from Lincoln to Chester got under way.

AD 78: Annexation of Brigantia. Agricola's advance up the east and west sides of the Pennines brought to completion work begun by Cerialis. The winter months of this and doubtless other years were spent advancing the Romanisation of the province in terms both of civil construction and of encouraging the adoption of a Roman lifestyle by the native nobility.

AD 79: Advance to the Forth-Clyde line, and beyond it, in the east, to the Tay.

AD 80: Consolidation of the Roman hold on lowland Scotland. At this point the advantages of the Forth-Clyde line as a viable frontier were recognised. Many advocated its adoption; Agricola insisted upon further advance. Who was right?

AD 81: Penetration of SW Scotland, an area by-passed in the initial push north. Agricola became aware of Ireland and was later to claim it could easily be held by Roman forces.

Very recently a Roman-style fort containing coins from the reigns of Titus to Hadrian - AD 79-138 - has in fact come to light to the north of Dublin. This was probably a defended port of entry for trade between Rome and the Irish which also served a political function, maintaining friendly relations with tribes and ensuring that such relations remained friendly.

AD 82: The move north was resumed, this time exclusively by the east coast route owing to the impenetrable terrain in the west. Advancing forces were supplied by sea, and the navy was used to terrorise coastal areas ahead of the army. The Caledonians united to resist and created disquiet among the Romans by attacking forts. The earlier dispute over where to call a halt resurfaced as the enemy adapted its tactics to take advantage of Roman weaknesses: when Agricola divided his forces to deal with dangers on a number of fronts, the enemy massed for an attack on a single Roman contingent.

AD 83: The terror-tactics of the fleet convinced the Caledonians to risk everything in a set battle at Mons Graupius under the leadership of Calgacus. In the engagement Agricola employed only auxiliary forces, keeping his legions in reserve. Although the enemy held the higher ground, superior Roman tactics and discipline won the day but were unable to annihilate the enemy, who melted away into the Highlands. As a final gesture Agricola instructed his fleet to sail round the top of Britain to demonstrate that it was indeed an island. He himself led his troops south into winter quarters and, following his recall to the continent, settled into retirement.

The battle at Mons Graupius meant defeat for the Caledonians, but was it really a victory for Rome? Agricola held the coastal plain north of the Tay, but was this an economically viable area that could be held against raids from the Highlands without committing huge forces to man forts at the mouths of the glens? Could four legions which had occupied the land up to Brigantia cope with a now-doubled area? What was possibly a hopeless task in 83 became demonstrably impossible when in subsequent years the II Adiutrix legion and auxiliary units were withdrawn for operations in Dacia (Romania), and a steady withdrawal from Scotland got underway. Inchtuthil on the Tay, the most northerly of the legionary fortresses established in Britain, was abandoned, and by the time of Hadrian the frontier was essentially based back on the Tyne-Solway line. Further south the fortresses at York, Caerleon and Chester were consolidated in stone, itself a highly indicative move, while the former fortresses of Lincoln and Gloucester were converted into colonies. With the arrival in Britain of Hadrian himself in AD 122 the scene was set indeed for further consolidation.

For a discussion of the Hadrianic and Antonine frontiers see Chapter 4.

The Severan Period (Herodian II 1-3, III 5-7, 14, Dio LXXV 6-7, LXXVI 13-15)
The problems of internal security which were probably responsible for the failure of the Antonine wall continued well into later decades of the 2nd century. In 163 we hear of the prominent military figure Calpurnius Agricola being sent to quieten the province, and further problems followed in 180 with a major incursion of barbarians across one of the walls (Dio does not specify which), resulting in the loss of a general and his troops. The loss was in fact severe enough for the

emperor of the day, Commodus, to send Ulpius Marcellus as governor. Despite reports of severe defeats inflicted on the enemy, Marcellus' excessive devotion to discipline, together with increasingly erratic policies coming from Rome, served merely to create further difficulties inside the province, rousing the troops themselves to near rebellion. When they attempted to appoint one of their own officers, Priscus, as emperor, Commodus' praetorian prefect Perennis countered by appointing as legionary commanders men whose social standing seemed calculated to humiliate the troops. As a result the legions sent a deputation to Italy which sowed enough seeds of doubt in Commodus' mind as to Perennis' ultimate ambition that the prefect's downfall was assured. In 185, to restore morale in the province Commodus sent a new governor, Helvius Pertinax, but he, like Marcellus, proved too much a disciplinarian to be accepted by the troops and following a severely punished attempt on his life by them he was driven from office.

After the death of Commodus in 192, and a brief reign by Pertinax, the imperial throne once again became the prize in a trial of strength. The Imperial Guard were content to auction the office of emperor to the highest bidder - Didius Julianus - but the true strength of the empire lay with the legions on the frontiers, and it was here that three contenders arose: Clodius Albinus, governor of Britain, Pescennius Niger in Syria, and Septimius Severus in the northern Balkans province of Pannonia. Severus' closeness to the heart of the empire and the superiority of his military support allowed him to steal a march on his rivals by the seizure of Rome, where the hapless Didius was sacrificed to the not-so-tender mercies of his former supporters. By according Albinus the rank of Caesar, which carried with it the promise of a share in government and the implication of succession, Severus was free to concentrate on his main enemy, Niger. Once the latter was out of the way an assassination attempt upon Albinus was enough to convince him that Severus was not interested in sharing power, and that he must instead stake everything on an invasion of Gaul and a fresh civil war. After an initial victory for Albinus against Severus' general Lupus the final showdown came in 197, close to Lyons. Although Dio clearly inflates the scale of the fighting, there can be no doubt that it was a hard-fought contest, but it left Albinus dead and Severus secure at last on the throne. In Britain itself Albinus' withdrawal of troops for service on the continent must have led to a serious power vacuum which his Severan successor Virius Lupus was hard pressed to fill. The north in particular seems to have been particularly vulnerable. Even if we accept that the subsequent widespread process of rebuilding in the area was undertaken to repair deterioration caused by time rather than enemy action, Dio's report of payments made to the Maeatae (the federation of tribes to the north of the frontier), in order to keep them quiet and prevent their alliance with the Caledonians, certainly indicates Roman weakness. When in 206-7 another governor, Alfenus Senecio, suggested an imperial visitation to quieten continuing unrest - and it must have been severe for Senecio even to make the suggestion - Severus did not refuse.

In 208 Severus arrived in the province with both his family and his court. While his younger son Geta was left to administer the day-to-day affairs of imperial government, the emperor and his elder son Caracalla brushed aside attempts at negotiation by the northern tribes and moved into Scotland. Even discounting the exaggerated details of Dio, the campaign of 209 in the territory of the Caledonians was no easy matter, with native resistance compounded by the difficulty of the terrain. Moreover, Severus himself was in rapidly declining health. Nevertheless victories were claimed and terms imposed on the local inhabitants. In 210, however, the Maeatae revolted and were joined by their northern neighbours the Caledonians when the Roman response threatened genocide. During the ensuing winter Severus' preparations for yet another campaign were cut short by his death at York on February 4th. In his haste to secure power for himself Caracalla is reported to have made a speedy peace with the enemy and to have begun pulling back to Hadrian's Wall. Within months the bad blood between the two brothers, now joint emperors, resulted in Geta's assassination, an event that seems to have been deeply resented in Britain. Despite this, the Severan strengthening of the northern frontier by widespread reconstruction, and Caracalla's settlement with the northern tribes, do ostensibly seem to have prevented any major upset in Britain for the next 80 years. Where problems did arise, they were either the result of external threats - raids by Saxon and Frankish pirates - or of imperial power struggles in the form of (1) the breakaway Gallic Empire established by Postumus in Gaul, Spain and Britain, which lasted from AD 260-274; (2) the abortive attempt by Bonosus to re-establish it in the time of the emperor Probus (276-82); and (3) a rebellion in Britain led by an unnamed governor, again in the reign of Probus. These secessionist movements were in fact reactions to the weakness that characterised central government in the decades between 244 and 284, as one emperor succeeded another with disturbing rapidity. Two major changes, however, did have an impact. At some stage either under Severus or Caracalla the province was divided in two (Fig. 11): *Britannia Superior* in the south, *Britannia Inferior* in the north, a division designed to prevent the island's forces being concentrated into the hands of one man, as in the case of Clodius Albinus. The fact that little is known of the governors who came and went in the succeeding decades itself points to the success of the policy and the stability of the area. The second change was in the growing cohesion within society between occupying Roman and native population brought about by (1) Caracalla's edict of 212 granting citizenship to all free inhabitants of the empire who still lacked that status, and (2) allowing soldiers to take legal wives (previously any union they formed with native women was not recognised in law until retirement).

Carausius and the Diocletianic Restoration
In 284 the instability that had rocked the empire for 40 years ended with the accession of Diocletian. Two years later he took Maximian as his fellow Augustus (now the title assumed by emperors), and assigned to him control of the western provinces. To meet the growing threat of Saxon and Frankish raids on the coast of Gaul Maximian in turn appointed Carausius to command the *Classis Britannica*, the British fleet. Soon, however, Carausius fell under suspicion of using his position for personal enrichment by intercepting raiders only after the event and not returning all the booty recovered. Rather than face the death sentence that surely awaited him, therefore, he declared himself a separate emperor in NW Gaul and Britain. The apparent absence of any resistance to such a move on the part of at least two of the legions in Britain suggests either that Carausius had already built up a following there, or that he was able to exploit continuing grievances against central authority among the troops. We cannot even be sure of any justification there may have been in the charge. The kind of military operations being carried out by the Saxons and Franks always gave the initiative to the raider - interception before the event must have been the exception not the rule - and the times were such that suspicion was enough virtually to guarantee condemnation. From vague references amidst the purple prose of the sources Maximian's initial reaction, attempted naval intervention in 288-9, seems to have been thwarted either by defeat or by bad weather, forcing him to buy time through a pretended recognition of Carausius' claim to legitimate authority. That such recognition was but a sham is shown by the fact that whereas

Carausius subsequently issued coins proclaiming the triple division of power, neither Maximian nor Diocletian returned the honour.

In 293 the division of power between Diocletian and Maximian was widened further when each took a deputy or Caesar, thus dividing the empire into four. To Maximian's deputy, Constantius, fell the north-west, including the provinces controlled by Carausius. Understandably, Constantius' first moves were directed against the usurper's continental territory and were a total success - enough of a blow to Carausius' prestige, in fact, to bring about his assassination and replacement by his finance minister, Allectus. After three years' preparation the time for the push into Britain itself arrived. Two fleets converged on the island. The first was commanded by Constantius himself and headed for the south-east; the other was under his praetorian prefect Asclepiodotus, his target the Solent. Although Allectus' main weapon was his own fleet, fog in the Channel prevented its use against Asclepiodotus, who burned his boats on landing as a sign of earnestness and marched inland. Only that same fog prevented the simultaneous arrival of Constantius' contingent. In the event this did not matter; for when battle was eventually joined, the usurper fell with many of his troops, a large percentage of whom were apparently Frankish mercenaries. The survivors headed for London to make good their escape overseas, but here they were intercepted and destroyed, following the timely arrival of Constantius' forces.

By the following year, 297, the situation in Britain had become sufficiently stable to allow Constantius to return to the continent. In 305 Diocletian and Maximian retired, and in 306 it was as Augustus that Constantius returned to Britain to campaign in the north. The motive for the expedition and its course, however, remain tantalisingly lost. That same year the emperor died at York, and on his death the empire once again lapsed into a feud of contending rivalries, the ultimate victor in which was Constantius' son, Constantine, elevated to the rank of Augustus by his father's troops in Britain. Meanwhile, at some stage before 314 the provinces of Britain had once again undergone reorganisation to bring them into line with changes that had already occurred on the continent. Britain now constituted a Diocese headed by a Vicar, a deputy of the Praetorian Prefect, and was subdivided into four provinces, each governed by a Praeses (Fig.11): *Britannia Prima* and *Britannia Maxima Caesariensis* formed out of *Britannia Superior*; *Britannia Secunda* and *Britannia Flavia Caesariensis* out of *Britannia Inferior*. Multiplication of provincial administration, however, was to bring with it its own problems, not least the expense of additional personnel. Nevertheless the early 4th century appears to have been one of unprecedented prosperity for Britain, as evidenced by public and private building on a lavish scale, especially at York itself, where the riverside fortifications were rebuilt in spectacular fashion. At some stage too there was a division between military and civil authority. Vicars and Praesides continued to control civil affairs, but command of the army passed to Dukes in the case of the diocesan garrison, and to a Count of the Saxon Shore in the case of the troops who manned the eastern and southern coastal defences (see pp. 49-51 below). Additionally, in the context of the whole empire Britain's forces were now designated *Limitanei*, frontier forces, as opposed to the *Comitatenses* or mobile field army that was deployed to troublespots on the continent.

The Dynasty of Constantine (Eusebius De Vita Constantini, Libanius Orations 18 & 59, Ammianus Marcellinus XVI, 5, XX, 1, XXX, 7)
While our literary sources reveal at least one subsequent visit to Britain by Constantine after 306, the date and circumstances remain unknown - the evidence of coins in fact suggests visits in 307, 312, and 314. It may also be to his reign that we should attribute additions to town defences or the construction of fortifications at previously undefended sites. This in turn implies the stationing of garrisons in such places and a policy-shift to one of defence in depth. The very nature of the undertaking suggests a considerable surplus in resources to finance it, and a belief that the towns of Britain were worth defending. The 6th century writer Zosimus criticises Constantine for the resultant move of troops from the frontiers of the empire to the towns, but the advent of far-ranging raiding parties made such local defence a practical necessity. On Constantine's death in 337 the empire was divided between his three sons, Constantius II who took the east, Constans to whom fell the central sector, and Constantine II who held the west, including Britain, and who in 340 invaded the territory of his brother Constans and was killed. By early in 343 the situation in the island had for some unspecified reason become serious enough to require a mid-winter visit by Constans. Our sources deny any pressing need; the mid-winter circumstances suggest otherwise, and vague hints point to the northern frontier as the focus of attention. Further unrest in Britain at some point before 350 is suggested by the presence there of the elder Gratian, who held the rank of *Comes*, Count, a title usually associated with the mobile continental field army. May we, therefore, suppose that he brought with him

detachments of such forces for some reason? In 350 Constans himself fell victim to the usurper Magnentius, who appears to have enjoyed enough support in Britain - not least perhaps because of his tolerant attitude towards paganism - to warrant an imperial investigation when Constantius II re-established control in 353. The leader of the commission, Paul, nicknamed 'the chain' because of his methods, rode roughshod over both individual rights and the amnesty that had been granted earlier. Such, in fact, was the havoc wrought in the diocese that when the Vicar's attempts to mitigate Paul's worst excesses failed, he resorted to attempted violence and then to suicide. Despite this, however, Britain continued to occupy an important position in the empire, not least because of its relative freedom from the external pressures now assailing the continental provinces. This made it, for instance, a valuable source of grain for the garrison of north-west Gaul and Germany, as the determination of Constantius' Caesar, Julian, to reopen the Rhine as a route for the transport of such grain displays. It was a matter of some urgency, therefore, when Britain suffered a large-scale attack by Picts and Scots (still an Irish tribe at this time) in 360. To rectify the situation Julian sent Lupicinus and four divisions of the continental field army. Of the campaign we know nothing and before long Julian's elevation to the position of Augustus caused him to recall and arrest Lupicinus in order to prevent him from siding with Constantius in the war now threatening between the two cousins, a threat only removed by the timely death of Constantius. By 363, however, Julian was himself dead and the dynasty of Constantine extinct.

The Decline of Roman Britain (Ammianus Marcellinus XXVII-XXIX, Gildas De Excidio Britanniae, Zosimus V-VI)
For Britain the 360s were a period of unprecedented danger. Ammianus (XXVI,4,5) refers to continuous harassment by Picts, Saxons, Scots and Attacotti in 364, perhaps no more than an oratorical flourish to highlight events on the continent. In 367, on the other hand, their concerted action produced the actual elimination of Britain's high-command with the capture of its supreme commander, the Duke Fullofaudes, and the death of Nectaridus, Count of the Saxon Shore. The emperor of the west, Valentinian, was too beset with problems to attend in person. Instead he sent in rapid succession first Severus, then Jovinus, before lighting on the right man for the job in the elder Theodosius. Bringing with him detachments of the continental army, Theodosius was able to begin recalling the battered

garrison to its ranks and to mop up the bands of barbarians roaming the countryside in search of loot. Indeed, the devastation they had produced underlined a chronic weakness in Britain's defences: the inability of the now static garrison to deal with an enemy that was both mobile and able to put into the field increasingly large forces capable of swamping individual positions piecemeal. Exacerbating the disaster in the north had undoubtedly been the actions of the Areani, who in the 2nd century had been known as *Exploratores*: forces stationed beyond Hadrian's wall to give advance warning of impending attack. Instead, they had now turned traitor and had supplied the enemy with information on Roman deployments. These men Theodosius removed from their positions altogether. It may also be to him that we should attribute construction of the signal stations along the Yorkshire coast from Huntcliff to Filey, and the addition of external bastions to town walls as the bases for Roman artillery. This in itself again suggests the stationing of small bands of troops to defend such civil settlements. When the situation began to stabilise - at least to the extent of Britain once again having a civil government in the shape of a new Vicar, Civilis, and a military chain of command headed by a Duke, Dulcitius - Theodosius introduced a new name to the island, Valentia, in honour of the emperor Valentinian. Whether this constituted the establishment of a fifth province or merely the renaming of an area, though, we cannot tell.

Although the intervention of continental forces might rescue Britain from its enemies, such contingents could not remain for ever, and once they left, the underlying weaknesses of the garrison were swift to re-emerge. Further attacks from the Picts and Scots came in 382, but though they were speedily dealt with by the then commander, Magnus Maximus, this led not to stability but to Maximus being elevated to the position of Augustus by his troops. Once this had been done, the usurper had no choice but to head to the continent and to stake his claim to control the whole of the western empire. For a time Maximus was successful, killing the legitimate emperor Gratian near Lyons and isolating his young brother, Valentinian II, in Italy. This too Maximus invaded in 387, forcing Valentinian to seek asylum with Theodosius, son of that earlier Theodosius who had rescued Britain. But Theodosius, who commanded the east, was in no mood to reach any accommodation with Maximus and in time destroyed him near Aquileia.

Maximus' continental adventure was probably inspired as much by a genuine feeling among his troops that the central government was blind to the problems of Britain as it was by personal ambition. Its effect, according to the later writer Gildas, was to denude the island of a large part of its garrison, which never returned. How true this is we cannot tell, and the reliability of Gildas is seriously open to question. He goes on, however, to record appeals sent from Britain and further contingents sent from the continent to drive out attacking Picts and Scots.

After the death of Valentinian II in 392 and that of Theodosius in 395 the western empire passed to Honorius, the younger of Theodosius' sons. In fact, however, actual control of government lay in the hands of the general Stilicho, and it was he who in the last years of the century sent further expeditions to Britain. For an empire fully stretched to defend its heartland the frequent need to divert forces to the periphery proved too great a burden and by 402 the flow of troops had become reversed, as forces were withdrawn from Britain to guard the continental provinces. Once again old grievances or acute nervousness as a result of external pressure seem to have awakened old solutions. During 407 usurpers were elevated in rapid succession and then toppled when they failed to live up to expectations: first Marcus, then Gratian, and finally Constantine III who, like Maximus before him, saw his future on the continent and eventually fell victim to the same fate in 411.

By this time imperial control in Britain had simply lapsed. What authority remained rejected the administration Constantine III had left behind and thereafter seems to have followed its own instincts. If the famous rescript of Honorius, granting the cities of Britain the right to take up arms for self-defence, does indeed refer to Britain, it marks a recognition that for the time being at least its citizens were on their own. In succeeding decades we hear of individual intervention by Germanus, who followed up his refutation of the Pelagian heresy (see Ch. 7) by leading the Britons to success against their enemies in the Alleluia victory. Similarly, Gildas, writing over a hundred years later, refers to appeals for Roman help between 446 and 454 in the face of increasing depredations from land and sea. With no help forthcoming the Britons found themselves increasingly squeezed between enemies from the north and Saxons who had been invited to settle along the east coast as a shield against the Picts. The Saxons, however, had not been slow to realise that what they received as pay they might seize by force, and the slow conversion of eastern Britain to England was under way.

Chapter 4
Soldiers, Forts and Frontiers

The evidence for military activity during the Roman conquest and occupation of Britain is particularly full compared with other parts of the Roman empire, and the province is interesting for the way in which it allows us to chart the processes of Romanisation, that is to say the interaction of Roman and native in the context of a gradual move away from military control to civilian order. Southern England and the Midlands were to develop a relatively high level of urbanisation, but the northern parts of the province were never demilitarised and urban life in those areas was conducted in a military environment throughout the period of Roman occupation. The military arrangements in Britain are also of special interest for the light which they cast on the development of thinking about the creation of bounds and frontiers for the empire as a whole. This phenomenon is nowhere better demonstrated than in north Britain on the lines of Hadrian's Wall and the Antonine Wall.

In order to understand the military dispositions in Roman Britain it is necessary to have a sense of how the Roman army itself worked. This account must therefore begin with a brief analysis of how the Roman army was organised. Traditionally, early in the Republic, the Roman army was an amateur, citizen-based, body which could be supplemented by drafts from the subject allies in times of trouble. From this situation there arose the long-standing distinction between the legions, or crack fighting troops, and the less highly regarded auxiliary units which did much of the work on the front line. By the time of Augustus there was a rough balance in the numbers of legionary and auxiliary soldiers. But the first century AD, which saw the conquest of Britain, also saw a continuing tendency for the numbers of auxiliaries to increase at the expense of numbers of legionaries as well as a tendency for legions and auxiliary units to be recruited from the provinces rather than from Italy as citizenship spread more widely throughout the empire. By the time of Hadrian legions were being recruited from provinces such as Gaul and Spain and from the Danubian territories, and the auxiliary units which manned Hadrian's Wall were brought from provinces in the eastern as well as the western empire.

In the later centuries of the Roman occupation of Britain the number of legions present in the province was reduced and new types of unit were introduced into the Roman military system. Amongst these were the *numeri*, which were, in effect, bands of tribesmen from frontier zones who were present in Britain by the early third century. They were recruited by compulsory levy under treaty arrangements, and the system of *numeri* was as much a way of controlling the territories from which the *numeri* were drawn as controlling the territory in which they were stationed. Thus in the second century *numeri* of British levies were active in Germany, and *numeri* of Sarmatian cavalry, from the Danube provinces, were stationed in northern Britain. In the fourth century *limitanei*, literally frontiersmen, who were a sort of farmer-cum-soldier, were established in the northern parts of the province.

TABLE 1: ORGANISATION OF THE LEGION

Basic Divisions of the Legion	
Contubernium	8 men
Century	10 contubernia
Maniple	2 centuries
Cavalry troop	120 men
Cohort I	5 double centuries
Cohorts II-X	6 centuries each

Size of the Legion			
1 Legion	10 cohorts and 1 cavalry troop		
Cohort I	5 double centuries	5 x 160	800
Cohorts II - X	6 centuries each	9 x 6 x 80	4320
Cavalry troop			120
Infantry centurions			59
Cavalry trooper			1
Total men in Legion			5300

The Legions
These were always the best-trained troops in any province and were very much seen as the Governor's strongest force and support. The strength of the legion was traditionally said to be 6,000 men. But legions were rarely at full strength, and the actual number in the field was probably closer to 5,000 than 6,000. The elements which made

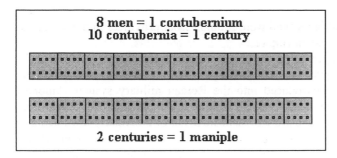

8 men = 1 contubernium
10 contubernia = 1 century

2 centuries = 1 maniple

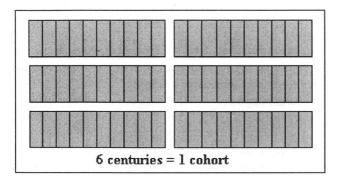

6 centuries = 1 cohort

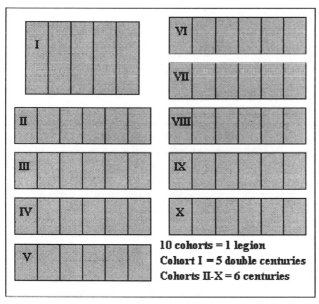

10 cohorts = 1 legion
Cohort I = 5 double centuries
Cohorts II-X = 6 centuries

Fig. 3 The elements of the Roman legion.

up the legion are illustrated graphically in Fig. 3. Table 1 gives the numbers of men which made up these elements. As well as the basic soldiers and officers, a legion would have contained numbers of special officers such as signal-bearers and personnel with particular skills, especially relating to engineering and medicine. It is unlikely that there would have been as many as 700 such people to bring up the size of the legion from the basic 5,300 to the traditional 6,000.

Each legion was commanded by a Legate (*legatus*), a Roman senator of praetorian rank, who was assisted by 10 military tribunes of equestrian rank, each in command of a cohort, but the backbone in the chain of command was provided by the 59 centurions, who were commonly promoted from the ranks. There were grades within the body of centurions, with the most senior (*primi ordines*) being in charge of the centuries of the first cohort and the first centuries of the other cohorts. The first centurion of the first cohort (*primus pilus*) was a figure of considerable importance in the legion as a whole.

Apart from the unit of 120 cavalrymen, the legionary soldiers were well armed and well trained professionals, more than a match for most of the relatively disorganised groups that they were likely to meet. They were citizens and were paid substantially more than their auxiliary equivalents, but the long term of service was a considerable disincentive to recruitment. Legionary soldiers could expect a grant of land upon discharge from the army, and these plots were commonly provided in the province in which the legion had been stationed. The effect of this system was to create clusters of citizen veterans in parts of the province, and these social groupings were an important factor in the process of Romanisation of the province.

The Auxiliary Units
Soldiers in the auxiliary units were not normally citizens, but became so on discharge after 25 years of service. There was therefore an incentive for provincials to join these forces, even though the pay and conditions of service were not as favourable as those enjoyed by the legionaries and, as has been seen, the auxiliary units rather than the legions were tending to expand in the early empire. Since the veteran auxiliaries often became attached to the women in the communities near which they were stationed, they tended to settle close to their former units and, like the legionary veterans, became part of the process of Romanising provincial territory.

Although less well regarded than the legions, the auxiliary units were still highly trained and very effective fighting forces, and it is clear that they bore the brunt of the fighting entailed by the conquest of Britain as well as providing the main part of the permanent garrison of the new province. Auxiliary units were both substantially smaller and considerably more variable than the legions. Most auxiliary units were about 500 men strong (quingenary) though there were also units of twice that size (milliary). Table 2 sets out the different types of auxiliary unit which could be comprised of infantry cohorts, cavalry *turmae*, or a mixture of both.

TABLE 2: ORGANISATION OF AUXILIARY UNITS			
Cohors quinge-naria peditata	Infantry cohort	6 centuries of 80 men	480 men
Cohors milliaria peditata	Double infantry cohort	10 centuries of 80 men	800 men
Ala quingenaria	Cavalry cohort	16 turmae of 32 men	512 men
Ala milliaria	Double cavalry cohort	24 turmae of 42(??) men	1008 men
Cohors quinge-naria equitata	Mixed cohort	6 centuries and 4 turmae	480 + 128(?) men
Cohors milliaria equitata	Double mixed cohort	10 centuries and 10 turmae	800 + 320(?) men

Auxiliary units were commanded by *praefecti* (quingenary units) and tribunes (milliary units): these were men of equestrian rank, and these military commands became part of a career structure which emerged for such men by the middle of the first century AD. Auxiliary units carried interesting titles which commonly recorded the name of the man who first raised the unit (e.g. *Ala Petriana* and *Ala Indiana*), or else indicated the original ethnic origin of the men (e.g. *cohors I Thracorum*). The units with specific ethnic titles were often those in which there were specialist troops, like the Hamian archers from Syria who were stationed at Carvoran on Hadrian's Wall. The ethnic titles tended to survive, even after the original recruits had been discharged. Normally only the officers would be Roman citizens, and units were stationed away from home presumably as a matter of policy. Thus we read in Tacitus (*Agricola*, 28) of the cohort of Usipi who were raised in Germany and stationed in Britain. The cohort murdered a centurion and some soldiers who were posted with them as instructors.

As Britain was settled, the auxiliary troops became, for practical purposes, the most effective provincial policing unit, offering to recruits, sometimes sons following their fathers, a secure career with citizenship at the end.

The distinction between legionaries and auxiliaries was not always totally clear. During the invasion period mixed forces were used in the field and it is clear, for instance, that the Roman unit which occupied the hillfort at Hod Hill was a vexillation consisting of both legionary and auxiliary soldiers. Such combined units can be attested from other vexillation fortresses, such as Longthorpe, which were constructed later in the first century. By the second century there was relatively little difference in terms of conditions of service between the legionaries and auxiliaries apart from rates of pay and the bounty on retirement. It is important always to remember that soldiers' duties consisted of much more than fighting and guard duties. They provided the main police force for the country and acted as bodyguard for imperial officials; they collected taxes and other levies from the civilians, and they were skilled labourers and engineers who constructed roads, bridges and aqueducts.

From the late second century onwards soldiers were allowed to marry, and even before then they had concubines who followed their units. These women and their families lived in the *vici* which grew up beside the forts and became a strong incentive for veterans to settle in the areas where they were based at the end of their military careers. In the last years of the Roman occupation of Britain the distinction between soldier and civilian seems to have become very blurred indeed, and finds of personal items such as jewellery and toys from forts like Housesteads and Wallsend show how families appear to have been housed inside the forts in the rows of chalets which replaced the traditional barrack blocks. A second century tombstone from South Shields at the mouth of the Tyne bears poignant testimony to the ways in which serving soldiers were assimilated into British society. This stone commemorates Regina, a freedwoman of the tribe of the Catuvellauni, wife of Barates. Barates was a Syrian from Palmyra whose unit was presumably stationed in southeast England. He would have acquired Regina as a concubine before he was moved up to Hadrian's Wall where she was given her freedom and he married her, presumably after discharge. Though of British birth, Regina is depicted in the Palmyrene manner as a high-ranking lady, enthroned in a grand chair and showing her jewel box and other private possessions. The tombstone of Regina is also of interest for showing how the unit at South Shields maintained its Syrian traditions and must even have contained a Palmyrene sculptor.

The Classis Britannica

Since Britain is an island, the Roman occupationary force needed a fleet. In the first century this was actually based at Boulogne, but during the second century another base was constructed at Dover. The fleet was a vital force during the invasion and in the first century was much in use for supplying the army as it moved forward under successive governors into the southwest, Wales and north Britain, and was heavily involved in the construction of Hadrian's Wall. It was traditionally seen as having inferior status to the land-based forces but became more important during the third century when the need for naval defence along the Saxon Shore was acute.

Military bases

The camps and forts in which the army was housed owed their plans to the traditions which developed early in the Republic when the armies raised to meet various emergencies were kept in tented enclosures. A Roman army on campaign would always construct a temporary camp for the night, whilst more permanently stationed units were placed in forts (auxiliary units) or fortresses (legions) when settled down in winter quarters. The distinction between the temporary camp and the not-so-temporary fort is an important one to grasp, but even legionary fortresses were often constructed from turf and timber and intended for months rather than years of occupancy. It was not until the early second century, the era that saw establishment of permanent frontiers, that stone-built forts, intended for lengthy occupancy, began to be constructed in Britain.

Camps

Camps were constructed by armies on the move in order to provide some protection from surprise attack during the night. They were simple earthworks consisting of ditch and banks and varied enormously in size (Fig. 4), according to unit and date, from small practice camps (on Llandrindrod Common and Gelligaer Common in Wales; and at Haltwhistle Burn and outside the hillfort of Birrenswark in Dumfriesshire in the general vicinity of Hadrian's wall) through to the huge marching camps, like Kirkbuddo, which were constructed during the Severan campaigns in Scotland and cover as much as 66 hectares (more than three times the extent of most

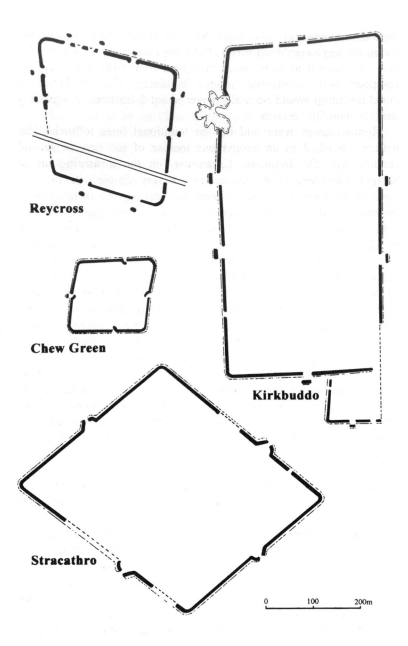

Fig. 4 Comparative plans of Roman marching camps (after Breeze).

legionary fortresses). The huge Severan camps were presumably meant for large combined forces, but camps were commonly smaller than the equivalent forts, since they held only tents and were not equipped with substantial service buildings. Thus a legionary marching camp would normally cover about 8 hectares, a legionary fortress about 20 hectares.

Roman camps were laid out on traditional lines following the pattern described in an anonymous treatise of the first or second century AD, *De Metatione Castrorum* (on the measuring-out of camps). The plans of Roman camps are very simple with most of them consisting of quadrilateral linear defences (square, rectangular or rhomboidal) with curving corners and one or more 'gates' on each side. The defences consisted of a ditch (*fossa*) which was a minimum of 5 Roman feet (1.48 m) wide and 3 Roman feet (0.89 m) deep, and a rampart (*vallum*) at least 8 Roman feet (2.37 m) wide and 6 Roman feet (1.77 m) high. The rampart was constructed from the soil dug out of the ditch and topped by a timber palisade made from the stakes each soldier carried. Camp gates were basically holes in the running banks protected either by simple *titula*, which were straight stretches of bank outside the openings (see the plans of Reycross and Kirkbuddo on Fig. 4), or curving extensions to the bank known as *claviculae*. These latter are often referred to as the Stracathro type (Fig. 4) after the site in Perthshire where they were first detected. The *clavicula* type of gateway was popular in camps belonging to the Flavian period and stylistic comparisons between marching camps can be used to show how the army was moving during, say, the campaigns of Agricola.

Inside the camps there are rarely any detectable signs of interior arrangements, but we know from the *De Metatione Castrorum* that the tents were organised in regular lines with the Officers' tents in a central position, the camp itself being divided up by internal 'roads'.

Marching camps are often detected from aerial photographs, and such photographs regularly show overlying marching camps (as on Gateshead Common) belonging to widely distant periods. This sort of evidence demonstrates that Roman military surveyors had fixed ideas about the suitable siting of marching camps rather than that they carried with them atlases showing sites for military bases.

Apart from special cases like the tiny practice camps thrown up by units in training and construction camps used by units which were building forts and fortresses or frontier works, camps were normally occupied for one night only and were thrown up at the end of the day's march. Every Roman soldier on the march had to carry the equipment for trenching and digging as well as the pair of wooden stakes which were used to form part of the palisade overnight. The daily task of constructing such camps appears unduly laborious, but from analysis of such camps as Reycross, where traces of internal arrangements give clues to the size of the occupying unit and therefore indicate the ratio of soldiers to each metre of perimeter, it can been estimated that if half the soldiers were committed to constructing the defences, each man would have had to excavate and deposit about one cubic metre of soil each day. This was not too arduous a task and this disposition of men would have left the rest of the men free to erect the leather tents on the traditional lines laid down, and which were to be used in turn for the more permanent forts and fortresses. Thus the *striga*, consisting of two rows of tents with a pathway between and space for the larger centurions' tents at one end, was to provide the model for the arrangement of barrack blocks in the forts. Construction of the camps required meticulous organisation rather than excessive labour, and the vast numbers of temporary camps known to have been constructed in Britain are testimony to the incredibly effective training and discipline of the Roman army in the field.

Forts
The terminology for the essential parts of a Roman fort (Fig. 5) was derived directly from that used to describe the layout of marching camps.These, as we have seen, were based on the traditional alignments of such camps with four linear defences, each broken by gateways, and internal arrangements based on the traditional rows of leather tents. The *via sagularis*, or *intervallum* street (i.e. street inside the rampart) ran round the perimeter, and the forts were divided into zones by their internal road systems. The front part of the fort, before the headquarters building (*principia*) and the *via principalis*, was thus known as the *praetentura* and the rear section was the *retentura*. The *principia* (Fig. 5.1) was the administrative focus of the fort: the central room at the back of the principia was the *aedes* or *sacellum*, the shrine of the unit where the standards and the image of the emperor were kept. Announcements were made in the hall of the *principia*, which contained a *tribunal* or platform for the commanding officer to address his troops. Disciplinary hearings were held, and soldiers were paid here - thus there was a pit or crypt in the

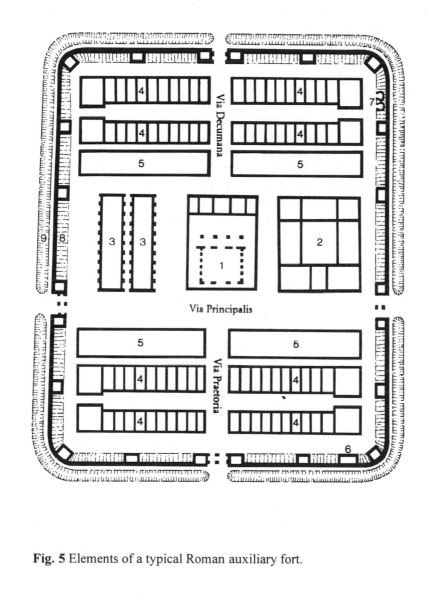

Fig. 5 Elements of a typical Roman auxiliary fort.

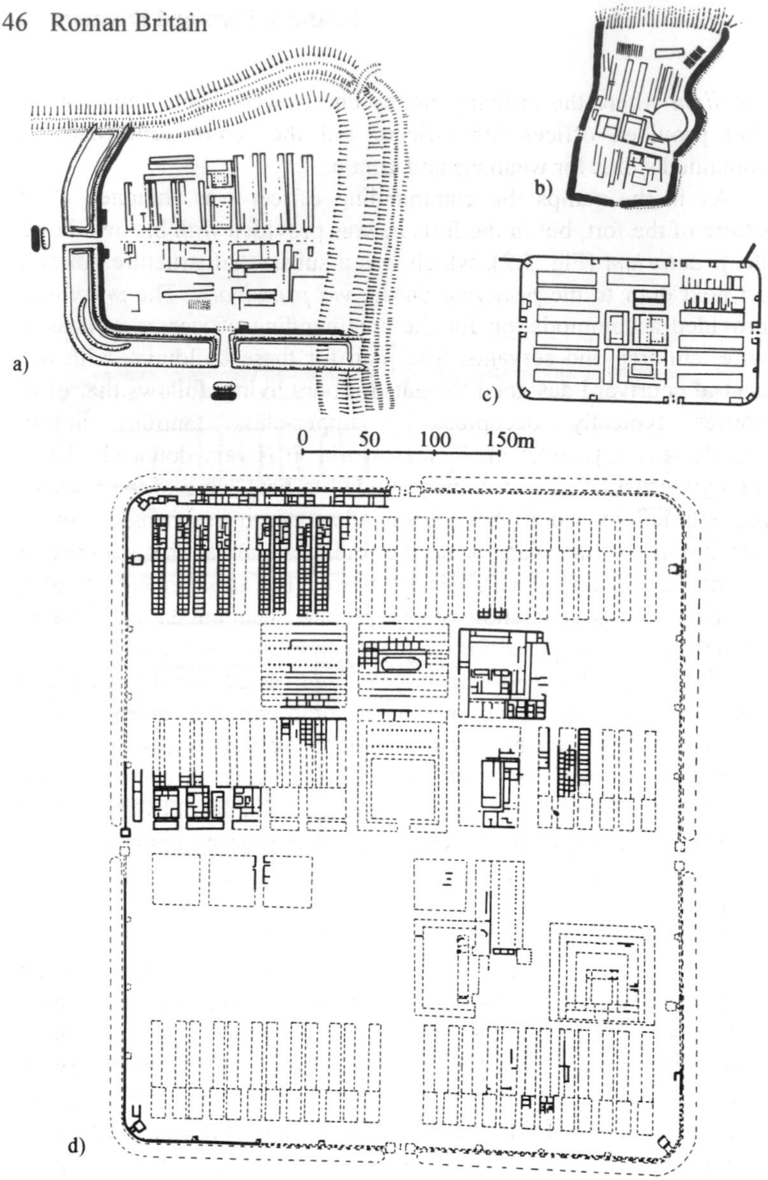

Fig. 6 Comparative plans of forts and fortresses.
a) Hod Hill, Claudian earth-and-timber invasion fort for a
mixed garrison, occupying a corner of the Iron Age hillfort; b) The Lunt, Baginton, c. AD 64 turf-and-timber fort
for a mixed garrison; c) Housesteads, stone-built Hadrianic
Wall fort for an infantry unit; d) Caerleon, c. AD 100 stone-
built legionary fortress.

sacellum where the military money chests were kept. The *principia* also provided offices for officers and the senior centurions and contained stores for weapons and armour.

As in the camps the commanding officer was stationed at the centre of the fort, but in the forts he was provided with his own house, the *praetorium* (Fig. 5.2), which was a substantial structure normally set next door to the *principia* on the *via principalis*. The *praetorium* provided accommodation for the commanding officer as well as his wife, children and servants. The plan for these buildings, with their central courtyard designed for out-of-doors living, follows that of the houses typically occupied by upper-class families in the Mediterranean parts of the Roman world. It is very doubtful whether the hypocaust heating systems provided to heat some of the rooms in these buildings would have been adequate to compensate for the unsuitability of the plan for northern climes such as that experienced by the Roman army in Britain. However, the arrangement of rooms did allow for a separation of the private accommodation from the formal chamber required for the reception of official visitors.

The final buildings on the *via principalis* were normally granaries, *horreae* (Fig. 5.3). There were most commonly two in an auxiliary fort, which were presumably sufficient to contain enough corn to see the brigade through the winter since Tacitus tells us in the *Agricola* that this was the normal level of provision maintained by the army of occupation. The granaries were long rectangular buildings raised on piers to discourage the entry of vermin and to ensure ventilation of the corn which was stored in bins and sacks inside the building.

The rest of the fort (i.e. the *praetentura* and *retentura)* was occupied by ranges of barrack blocks (Fig. 5.4), as well as stables and workshops (Fig. 5.5). The latter were simple rectangular structures, with stables often being distinguished by the provision of open drains along one side of the building. Each barrack block held a century and consisted of ten rooms which normally had an ante-room for equipment ranged along a verandah. The centurion had larger chambers at the end of the barrack block with a view along the verandah. The centurions' rooms were normally at the end of the barrack block which was nearest to the rampart, perhaps because a missile projected into the fort would tend to be aimed over the top of the rampart and was therefore likely to strike some way down the barrack block towards the interior of the fort. (Barrack blocks with rows of eight or nine rooms are found in cavalry forts). The rear rooms in which the men slept were normally about three metres square. This is a small area for eight men, and it seems likely that the practice of 'warm-bedding' must have been in operation with maximum occupancy of beds being achieving by soldiers who were on different watches using the same beds at different times during the day. Although early forts (e.g. Hod Hill and the Lunt) sometimes had barrack blocks with rows of single rooms, the system of having two rooms for each *contubernium* rapidly became standard in Roman Britain, and it may well be the case that the simpler, more constricted, early barrack blocks reflected conditions during the early years of the invasion. At the end of the third century, or the beginning of the fourth, there was a shift from communal rows of barrack rooms to rows of nearly detached chalets. The change would appear to suggest that there were less men in the centuries and also that families were perhaps allowed inside the forts.

Other structures found in forts are concerned with a variety of activities which were essential for the soldiers' well-being and the provision of necessary equipment. Such structures would include hospitals, usually near the centre of the fort, and latrines and ovens which for practical reasons were regularly tucked into the back of the rampart. Bath-houses were usually provided outside the forts, so as to be near suitable water supplies.

Compared with camps, forts were normally — though not invariably — more regularly planned, following the standard playing-card shape and were usually more precise in their internal arrangements. Those, such as Fendoch, which are associated with the Flavian move into Scotland are good examples of regular fort-planning and provide the model, for instance, for their stone successors which were constructed along the line of and in the vicinity of Hadrian's Wall. Exceptions to the rule that forts were highly regular can often be explained by peculiar local circumstances relating to topography or function. Thus the Roman fort at Hod Hill (Fig. 6a), demonstrates very well the changes to the norm which could arise from circumstances. It was tucked into the northwest corner of a native hillfort in the first years of the invasion and was occupied by a mixed vexillation of legionary infantry and auxiliary cavalry, with six legionary barrack blocks on the south side of the fort and six auxiliary cavalry blocks on the north side. Since the original Iron Age defences were standing, the Roman soldiers constructed ditches and ramparts only on the south and east sides.

In the case of the Lunt, near Coventry (Fig. 6b), the site was first occupied by a vexillation fortress and at some date in the first century, probably after the end of Boudicca's rebellion, was much reduced in size and to judge from the *gyrus*, a circular structure probably designed for breaking-in horses, used as a training centre for the cavalry. The western and more particularly the eastern ramparts at the Lunt curved round external and internal features rather than observing the straight lines which are normal in Roman forts. It is easy to believe that the walkway at the top of the curving eastern rampart would have provided an excellent viewing point for watching demonstrations in the *gyrus*.

Throughout most of the first century forts were constructed with turf ramparts and timber buildings. Such materials imply that that these forts were regarded as relatively impermanent structures, although the experiment of reconstructing the turf rampart and timber buildings of the Lunt has shown that with sensible maintenance programmes it is possible to keep such structures in use for thirty years or more. The shift to stone construction which came at the end of the first and the beginning of the second century marks a shift in thinking about the occupation of Britain towards the assumption that boundaries were becoming defined and the pattern of Romanisation was settling into a system where civilian rule applied through the southern parts of the province, whilst a strong level of military control was to be retained in the frontier zones. With this shift in thinking came a need for more permanent military bases which could be more easily maintained and in these circumstances the extra expense of creating stone-built forts was a worthwhile investment. At first the shift to stone construction was marked by no change in terms of the planning and siting of forts. This is perhaps surprising since the first century forts were essentially offensive structures with wide gateways designed for easy egress of troops, and towers which provided a view of the surrounding countryside. These early forts were convenient wintering quarters which provided protection against the northern weather, but would not have been suitable for sitting inside during prolonged sieges. They tended to be sited on level ground with control of important lines of communication, whether by road or river, and are not normally found in high easily defended positions. With time, however, the emphasis did become more defensive. The third and fourth century forts which were constructed along the Saxon Shore (Fig. 7) moved away from the playing-card shape and relatively slight defensive ramparts to plans which made much more use of the contours of the site and provided massive walls for effective

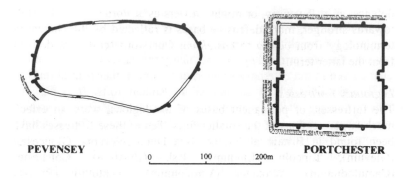

PEVENSEY   PORTCHESTER

0   100   200m

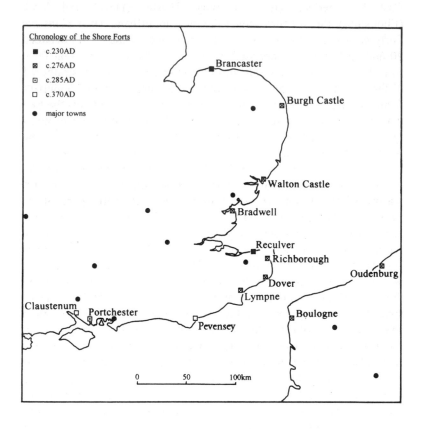

Fig. 7 The Saxon Shore Forts.

defence, as at Pevensey, or mighty towers as at Portchester. The shift towards stronger, more defensive bases is reflected by the change in terminology from *castra* to *castellum*. Our word 'castle' is derived from the latter term.

Legionary Fortresses

The fortresses, or permanent bases of the legions, were, in effect, much larger versions of the smaller forts. Ten of these fortresses have been found in Britain at Exeter (Isca Dumnoniorum), Gloucester (Glevum), Lincoln (Lindum), Usk (Burrium), Colchester (Camulodunum), Wroxeter (Viroconium), Inchtuthil (Pinnata Castra?), Caerleon (Isca Silurum), Chester (Deva) and York (Eboracum), the last three being the most long-lived. Their plans are fairly consistent and they are all distinguished by their size, between 20 and 22 hectares as opposed to the 1.5 to 2 hectares normal for a fort. Fig. 6, which shows all sites at the same scale, demonstrates the difference in size very graphically. The sites of most legionary fortresses are now occupied by modern towns. This reflects the fact that sites like Gloucester were handed over to civilian control when the legions moved on, but it also means that our understanding of the legionary fortresses is constrained by the fact that most of them have been encumbered with later buildings. However, the site of the Flavian fortress at Inchtuthil, probably intended for Legion XX Valeria Victrix, has never been built over and substantial parts of the fortress at Caerleon (Fig. 6d), built for Legion II Augusta, are also accessible. These two, accordingly, provide the best information about the internal layout of the legionary fortress. The surviving evidence suggests that, whilst the fortresses followed the main lines of the forts, with the same divisions by the *via principalis* and *via praetoria* and the *principia* still being placed at the centre, the general allocations of space were more generous. There were wider roads and more living space for the soldiers: the barrack blocks at Inchtuthil had 14 *contubernia* and those at Caerleon had 12. The centurions' quarters were also more generous, with the centurions of the first cohort having courtyard houses similar to the *praetoria* provided for the commanding officers of auxiliary units. Each cohort at Inchtuthil had its own granary. Unlike the forts, the legionary bases often had bath-houses provided inside the defences. The fortress at Caerleon measured 492 by 410 metres including the ramparts which consisted of stone walls nearly 2 metres thick backed by clay banks up to 7

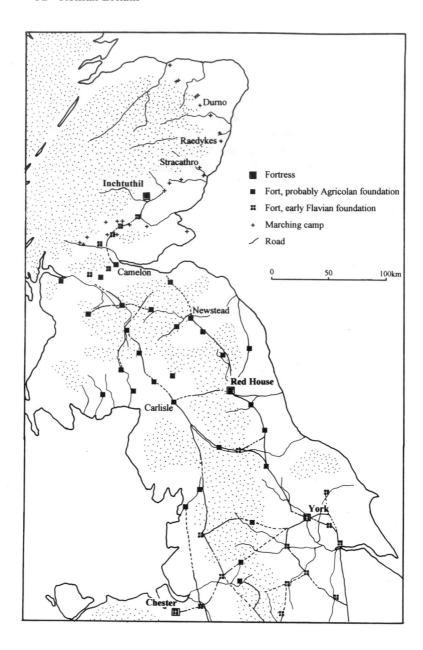

Fig. 8 Northern Britain under Agricola (after Breeze).

metres wide. There were probably 64 barrack blocks and an amphitheatre was constructed outside the fortress.

The Development of the Frontier in Roman Britain

In the first years of occupation after Claudius' invasion of Britain there seems to have been little thought of stopping the process of annexation. A series of road lines serve to indicate the progress of advance from time to time, but even though Boudicca's rebellion was a setback it is probably wrong to assume, as has been suggested, that the Fosse Way served as a frontier after AD 60. Such roads as the Fosse Way, which runs from Exeter to Lincoln, should rather be seen as part of the necessary system of military communication which was vital for securing occupied territory and for staging the advance further north. By 78 northern England was under Roman control and Agricola was moving into Scotland (Fig. 8). As a base for his supply lines Agricola established forts to control the road along the Stanegate line across the Tyne-Solway isthmus with major forts at Corbridge and Carlisle. Scotland as far north as the Forth-Clyde isthmus was occupied and Agricola then led campaigns towards the Highland zone. These Flavian campaigns were concerned with advance, but a prudent and cautious one and, by plotting the sites of the Agricolan forts in Scotland, it is possible to see how each campaign season ended with the establishment of appropriate wintering quarters. The best known Flavian forts in Scotland form a line from Loch Lomond across to Perthshire and forts such as Bochastle, Menteith and Fendoch were carefully positioned to control the drove-roads from the Highland glens. This northern Flavian line was in place by 85 and was centred on the legionary base at Inchtuthil. It was a double-edged system which could serve as a springboard for advance into the Highlands or could be used to protect the occupied territory of lowland Scotland from incursion by the Caledonian tribes.

By 87, however, because of strains on the continent in Germany and the Danube provinces, it became necessary to withdraw some troops from Britain. The combination of weaker military presence and continued insistent local resistance caused first the stopping of the process of advance in Britain and then the gradual withdrawal back to the Tyne-Solway line. The fortress at Inchtuthil and the various glen-blocking forts were soon abandoned and the army moved gradually south again, destroying some forts as it went but maintaining some others. It was perhaps during this period of consolidation that the frontier line along the Gask Ridge system in Perthshire was created with a series of towers set along the road line. Ultimately the bases at Carlisle and Corbridge where the main north-south roads crossed the Tyne-Solway line were re-occupied and the Stanegate became an important link with intermediate forts and fortlets added along the line. The process of consolidation continued into Trajan's reign (98-117), and this was the period which saw the conversion of forts and fortresses into permanent stone structures. The Gask and Stanegate lines were obviously created as part of the process of consolidation, and they may be seen as proto-frontiers, predating the next development which was the creation of the solid linear barrier of Hadrian's Wall.

Hadrian's Wall (Figs. 9 and 10)
The chronologies of the construction and occupation of Hadrian's Wall have long been the subjects of debate among scholars of the history of Roman Britain. Describing the wall is a relatively simple matter; defining its purpose is more controversial. It cannot be doubted that Hadrian's Wall represented a significant move away from Trajan's policy of general expansion of Roman territory, since the wall clearly marked a terminus, a point beyond which Roman rule was less direct. But it is not so clear that Hadrian's Wall should be defined in the military terminology of defence and offence. It seems hardly credible that it was ever meant to be a siege barricade, and the simple statement offered in the Augustan Histories (*SHA, Hadrian*, 5, 11, 2) that Hadrian 'was the first to build a wall, 80 miles long, to separate Romans and barbarians' may be as close as it is possible to get to the truth. Such a definition would conform with the purpose of frontiers in other parts of the Roman empire, though elsewhere the Romans made full use of natural barriers such as rivers and deserts. In the absence of such a natural line of demarcation in northern Britain, Hadrian made use of the narrow gap between the Solway on the west and the Tyne on the east as the basis for a mural defence which ran for 50 miles (80 Roman miles) across the country. Hadrian's line was either slightly north of or co-terminous with Trajan's Stanegate line, but whereas the Stanegate was an obviously convenient line of communication across northern England, which often used the river valleys, Hadrian wherever possible chose the high, visible ground for his wall.

Hadrian's Wall (Figs. 9 and 10) is the most important frontier monument known from the Roman period. It is 117 kilometres long, stands about 1.8 to 3 metres thick and was between 4.5 and 6.2 metres

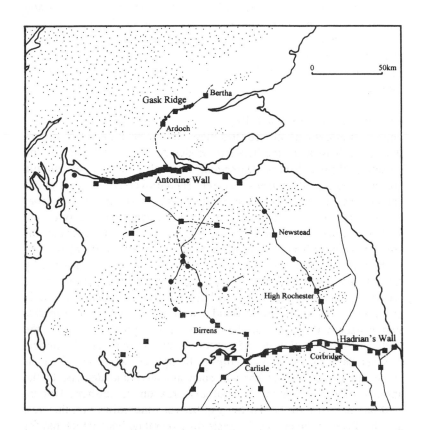

Fig. 9 Hadrian's Wall and the Antonine Wall (after Breeze).

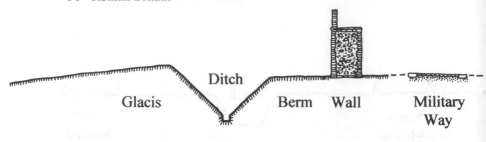

Fig. 10 Section through Hadrian's Wall.

high. The curtain wall alone, therefore, contained approximately 1.5 million cubic metres of building material. Hadrian's Wall transcended geography crossing a contrasting landscape of peak and valley, with three river-crossings, and the successful completion of an undertaking on this scale was at once a tribute to remarkable Roman organisation and a grandiose statement of power. Hadrian's Wall was not just a simple defensive wall. Whilst it was planned to take tactical advantage of the local geology and to provide a massive fighting platform should such be needed, it was also a central feature in a complex landscape which was to see 300 years of Roman activity much of which evolved as a result of its presence. In its final form Hadrian's Wall had 16 forts, plus a supply base at South Shields on the mouth of the Tyne, at least five outpost forts to the north, plus four forts and a range of smaller stations on the Cumberland coast. Fig. 10 shows the elements of the wall in its most complete form with the road (military way) protected by the wall itself and the wall ditch on the north side, and by the mounds and ditch of the *vallum* to the south.

Hadrian (reigned 117-38) combined the characteristics of scholar and soldier and, as the latter, made a tour of duty inspecting military zones in the empire. Trajan had pursued an aggressive expansionist policy, but Hadrian was committed instead to consolidation, establishing a palisade between the Rhine and the Danube and initiating the scheme for the Wall in Britain 'to separate Romans and barbarians'. Hadrian's Wall was planned to run on higher and more strategic ground than the Stanegate and its central section therefore occupied the Whin Sill, a soft fold of volcanic rock 10 miles to the north of the Stanegate, though a close relationship was maintained between the wall and the communications afforded by the road.

The first phase of construction was under way by 122 and continued until 124. The original plan for the wall was that it was to

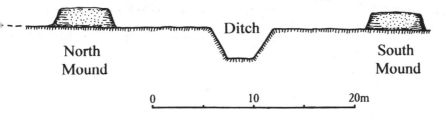

be built of stone between Newcastle and the river Irthing, whilst the remaining section to the west was constructed in turf and timber with a cobble platform where necessary.

Small fortlets at regular spacing, milecastles, were set at intervals of one Roman mile on the south side of the wall. At first most milecastles had gateways providing for travel through the wall and these fortlets therefore combined the roles of being controlled crossing points as well as providing accommodation for a limited garrison at close intervals along the system. Two stone turrets were provided between each pair of milecastles. These had no gates on their north side and can only have accommodated a very small number of soldiers.

The wall was constructed by teams from three legions which worked in stretches of 5-6 miles each. Formal inscriptions record construction of milecastles and smaller stones, normally set into the wall, mark the completion of a section by particular brigades.

Although the various units were clearly working to the same basic modules, sections of wall constructed by different legions display small differences in proportions and minor variations at a detailed level in the form of milecastles and towers.

Since it was the first attempt to create a permanent continuous frontier, it is not surprising that the plan for Hadrian's Wall was subject to modification during the period of its construction. It seems that the stone section of the wall was originally intended to have a width of about 10 Roman feet (2.96 metres - the 'broad wall'), but at an early stage the decision was taken to reduce this to about 6 Roman feet (1.78 metres - the 'narrow wall'). We know that the stone section of the wall was built from east to west because the east end has broad wall on broad wall foundation, but though broad wall gauge foundation was laid throughout the stone section, it was not always

used to its full width. The milecastles and turrets were also built in advance of the curtain wall as may be seen, for example, at Brunton Turret which has wings of broad wall gauge over which rises the subsequent narrow wall constructed in this section.

The western stretch of wall for the 48 kilometre section from the Irthing river crossing to Bowness was at first constructed from turf and timber, often on a cobbled foundation. The local stone in this area was considerably inferior to the limestone available in the eastern and central sectors, but the turf and timber proved to be a temporary solution since the western sector was replaced in Cumberland red sandstone. Although the milecastles were also constructed in turf and timber and stood on a broad base, the turrets were made of stone. The lack of wing walls on the western turrets suggests that there was no intention to bond the turrets with the subsequent stone curtain wall. When the western sector was reconstructed in stone, the wall mostly followed the original turf and timber line, with milecastles being rebuilt and the existing stone turrets incorporated into the system. In some places, as in the section west of Birdoswald fort, the stone wall deviated from the line of its turf and timber predecessor, and this has allowed archaeological investigation of the different stages of construction.

Although now nowhere higher than 3.3 metres, the wall was originally higher than that and may well have been crenellated as is suggested by the depiction on the Rudge cup, which was found in a Roman villa in Wiltshire and shows a castellated wall with inscriptions giving names of some of the forts on Hadrian's Wall. The external front of the wall consisted of coursed, squared limestone blocks which faced a rubble and mortar core. There is evidence to show that parts at least were rendered, inscribed with false pointing and whitewashed. Where the wall crossed rivers, near Carlisle, at Willowford and at Chesters, simple bridge abutments supported a structure which carried the curtain wall across the water on the same gauge as the rest of the system.

At first there appears to have been no intention to station forts on the line of Hadrian's Wall. Instead, accommodation was based on the Stanegate line between Corbridge and Carlisle which was also the base for supplies. The decision to add forts on the wall line was taken by about 126, although the Stanegate forts were also maintained. At first there were twelve such forts about 7.5 miles apart, and another four were built before the end of Hadrian's reign. All these forts conformed to the basic conventions current at the period, though some, like Benwell, straddled the wall and had six gates in all rather than the conventional four. The structural relationship between the wall and its forts can be seen at Housesteads where the building of the fort led to a slight re-alignment of the wall line and the suppression of a primary tower. The remains of this tower have been excavated, and can be seen just inside the north gate of the fort. The north gate at Housesteads also demonstrates how the army must have been driven by rigorous attention to the rule book, for this is a gate where none was needed: there is a steep drop immediately outside the fort wall at this point.

Contemporary with the provision of forts along the wall came the construction, to the south of the line of the wall, of the vallum. This consisted of a flat-bottomed ditch flanked by banks to north and south. The vallum runs basically parallel with the wall, but is sometimes very close, as at Benwell, and at other times, especially in the central sector, up to a kilometre away from the wall. Causeways with large free-standing gates were provided in the vallum where access to the wall was required. The vallum therefore controlled access to the south side of the wall and lends credence to the idea that there may have been some opposition to its presence from Brigantian natives living on the province side of the frontier.

Why was Hadrian's Wall built?

The purpose of Hadrian's Wall remains controversial. It was certainly a barrier, but was it meant to keep people in or out? Was it a defended and defensive fighting platform or a demarcation line where passage in both directions could be monitored and tolls and taxes could be collected? Did it, as the ancient writers say, simply mark out what was considered to be Roman? The answer probably lies in a combination of various of the propositions. The function of the wall probably changed from time to time, as is suggested by the reduction and ultimate closing of so many of the gates which allowed passage through the milecastles. It is clear from the archaeological evidence that watching and patrolling were important parts of military life in the wall zone. The turrets along the curtain wall between the forts are intervisible, and outpost forts were created in the territory to the north of the wall. Beyond the line of the wall proper, at the western end, a line of milefortlets and turrets was established along the Cumbrian coast. This was possibly strengthened by a timber palisade and a ditch and presumably served to control unauthorised access across the Solway Firth.

Like the forts built in Britain in the first century, Hadrian's Wall was surely not intended as a fighting platform to be defended in the event of 'siege' warfare, but was rather a structure providing temporary security in the event of movements from the north and a base for policing activity. It would have been relatively easily scaled, but with a comparatively small garrison of perhaps no more than 60 men in any one mile it would have prevented large-scale movements of people. In the real context that the Britons to the north of the Wall were more likely to have indulged in guerrilla tactics and hit-and-run raids than large-scale co-ordinated aggression, Hadrian's Wall would have been a more than adequate deterrent and protection against such border raids. It would have also served to control the passage of goods and people as well as being a very obvious statement of the strength of Roman arms and a disincentive to incursions into the province. Hadrian's Wall may have been the first major piece of evidence to show that the Roman empire had accepted that it had limitations, but it was in no way an admission of defeat, rather a very impressive statement of Roman authority. As has been seen, the function of the Wall seems to have changed with the passing of time. Although the gateways through the milecastles were blocked and the turrets fell into disuse, some forts were adapted to have three northern gates. Thus the balance between the function of the wall as a defensive barrier and its offensive capability was regularly shifting.

After Hadrian's death in 138 there was a renewed move to occupy southern Scotland under his successor Antoninus Pius (reigned 138-161). The move was cemented by the creation of the Antonine Wall, a turf and timber wall on the Forth-Clyde isthmus (see Fig. 9). This was built by the same legions as Hadrian's Wall and on the same design with milecastles, turrets and forts, but all on a smaller scale. Hadrian's Wall was not entirely abandoned but was rendered temporarily inoperative as a barrier since the gates of the milecastles were removed and parts of the vallum were back-filled. During the occupation of the Antonine Wall, Hadrian's Wall thus lost its role as a control point though it was still available as a support base.

The Antonine Wall was itself abandoned in about 157-8, probably in the context of the removal of troops from Britain to deal with troubles in Germany in the late 150s. Hadrian's Wall and the Stanegate forts were repaired and re-occupied in the 160s, and this phase saw the addition of the road known as the 'Military Way' (Fig. 10) behind the wall. There is, however, no evidence for the restoration of the vallum, a fact which probably reflected the increasing civilian activity in the neighbourhood of the Wall zone. Civilian communities grew up around the military bases, doubtless attracted by the large presence of troops with salaries to spend and the demands for supply of food and equipment supply. The *vici* (see p.67 below) beside the forts would have housed the common-law families of the soldiers and, as can be seen from the house outside the south gate of Housesteads fort which had a body walled up inside it, may have catered for other pursuits, some dubiously legal, which would have appealed to the military units but which were not available inside the forts.

The increasing interaction of soldier and civilian in the frontier zone shows how the process of Romanisation was active even in the furthermost reaches of the province. In the late 160s the forts at Corbridge and Carlisle were demolished and made into towns, as the civilian population was so extensive and the distinction between Roman soldier and native civilian became increasingly blurred. The logical end to this process came at the turn of the third and fourth centuries when the *Limitanei* (see p.31 above) who by then occupied the Wall zone brought their families to live in the wall forts with them.

It is difficult to define when Hadrian's Wall was given up. Although the Picts were an increasing problem in the 4th century, northern Britain was less and less a concern relevant to the Roman empire, and it seems that troops were removed to fight elsewhere more often than they were used to settle problems on the north frontier. By 410, when Britain was left to fend for itself, the soldiers who remained were more than ever like farmers and it is clear that some of the military installations inside the forts were used as dwellings and as pens for livestock.

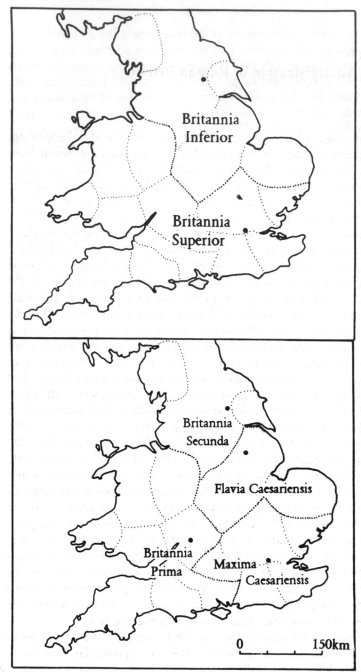

Fig. 11 Administrative Divisions of Roman Britain

Chapter 5
The Administration of Roman Britain

In the wake of conquest came the inevitable need to administer conquered territory. In this respect Britain proved no different from any other province of the Roman empire, and the means by which government of the island was carried out reflected what had long been practised elsewhere. Supreme responsibility in this, as in so much else, lay in the hands of the governor, the *Legatus Augusti Pro-Praetore*. Because of Britain's large military garrison he was regularly drawn from those members of the Senatorial order who had held the consulship, and was often specifically chosen because of some particular expertise which matched the Roman perception of the province's needs at the time. In the case of figures like Suetonius Paulinus, Petillius Cerialis or Agricola such talents were primarily military in nature. With Petronius Turpilianus or Trebellius Maximus in the decade after the Boudiccan rebellion the need was clearly more for reconstruction and regeneration. One man alone, however, does not constitute an administration, and to carry out central policy as laid down by the governor there was a large permanent staff either attached directly to the headquarters (originally in Colchester, later in London), or stationed throughout the province. For the most part the upper levels of this were manned by soldiers seconded from the legions and headed by a *Princeps Praetorii* of senior centurion rank. Under him operated the various grades of *Commentarienses*, whose duties included legal matters, *Cornicularii* (adjutants), *Speculatores* responsible for condemned prisoners and who also acted as official couriers, *Beneficiarii* who oversaw the organisation of supplies, maintenance of roads and posting stations, and *Stratores* who may have been connected with the supply of transport. Below these in turn was the inevitable staff of clerks - freedmen and slaves - who did the 'paperwork'. In addition to this official staff a governor would often also bring with him to the province an unofficial body of friends, his *cohors amicorum*, who acted as independent consultants.

However, notwithstanding personal strengths and the imperial policy of the day, the governor's area of responsibility was wide-ranging. When not actually campaigning, i.e. in the winter months, a governor would be expected to concentrate upon aspects of central administration as diverse as Romanising the local nobility and the construction of roads. One of the most important of these tasks was undoubtedly the administration of justice, something in which the governor would have had experience earlier in his career as praetor in Rome. In this field the governor constituted the final court of appeal for non-citizens (*peregrini*), was involved with all cases where there was the possibility of the death sentence or condemnation to the mines, and was expected to adjudicate appeals from decisions under native law. This last aspect must have been particularly onerous in the early days of the expanding province and explains the appointment in Vespasian's time (AD 69-79) of the *Legatus Juridicus* specifically to assist the governor in legal matters. Two early examples during the Flavian period, Gaius Salvius Liberalis Nonius Bassus and Lucius Iavolenus Priscus, were both prominent jurists, an indication of the importance attached to the post. Others like Marcus Vettius Valens, Gaius Sabucius Maior Caecilianus, or Marcus Antius Crescens Calpurnianus date from the time of Hadrian, Marcus Aurelius and Septimius Severus, when the need for the governor to be active in north Britain may have necessitated some such help in legal matters.

The one area where the governor's remit did not run, however, was the economic development of the province, which lay in the hands of the *Procurator Augusti Britanniae*, a man drawn from the lower, though still wealthy, Equestrian order. But though the procurator was socially inferior to the governor, he was not subject to him, and like him had direct access to the emperor and could on occasion act as a valuable corrective, as Classicianus did in the case of Suetonius Paulinus. We know the names of some ten procurators who served in Britain, but of their staffs there is little information. Analogy with other provinces, though, might suggest a wide-ranging body of junior procurators to oversee imperial estates, those mines not under direct military control, and taxation. Taxes within the province were relatively simple: the most important was the *annona* or corn-tax, grain bought for a nominal sum and used to feed the garrison and administration (cf. Tacitus *Agricola* 19). Others included the *tributum soli* on other produce of the land, the *tributum capitis*, a poll or property tax, and customs duties. In order to maintain accuracy of taxation periodic censuses took place and at least two names of those involved in them survive: Titus Statilius Optatus under Hadrian, and Marcus Arruntius Frugi under Antoninus Pius.

Local Government

For all its seeming complexity the central administration of Roman Britain was a far cry from the enormous bureaucracies of the modern state. Even so, while the governor from the capital or from his headquarters while on active service might oversee administration at the highest level, the province also needed a system of local administration to replace the tribal government that had operated before the invasion. In frontier areas where there was a legion military jurisdiction was an easy answer. Elsewhere, devolvement of government to a local level in areas where stability seemed assured brought an element of native involvement into the task of administration. An early, and essentially transient, stage is seen in the use of client-kings, who were relied upon to maintain the loyalty of their tribes, thus freeing Roman forces for use elsewhere. In return the tribe retained its native identity, laws, and the right to bear arms. The most successful of these kings was Cogidubnus of the tribe that came to be known as the Regnenses, with his capital probably at Chichester. Further north the Iceni typify the experiment that failed, largely owing to Roman heavy-handed treatment both in AD 48 and in 60. It is probable that the Brigantes under Cartimandua also had client status and here too the relationship broke down in the late 60s, though this time for more internal reasons.

The importance that Rome placed upon local autonomy is shown by the fact that the first recorded instance was established within six years of the invasion, with the conversion of the legionary fortress at Colchester into a colony (*colonia*). In terms of status the colony held prime position within local government, being essentially an urban settlement of legionary veterans - all of them Roman citizens - which controlled a considerable area of surrounding countryside (its *territorium*) made up of the farms given to the soldiers as part of their retirement grants. By the end of the century two more had been added - at Gloucester and Lincoln, again the conversion of redundant legionary fortresses into civil settlements and centres of Roman influence, intended to inspire and overawe the native populations in which they were situated. Later still, in the Severan period, the civil settlement that had grown up around York was similarly upgraded to the status of colony, as probably at some stage was London itself. The actual administration of the colony in many ways mirrored in miniature that of Rome, with a local Senate, the *Ordo*, made up of a hundred decurions, originally elected by the citizen body but who eventually became self-perpetuating in their office. Two executive officers, the *Duoviri Juridicundo*, presided over meetings of the *Ordo* and, as their name implies, regulated local justice as well as controlling the administration of festivals and other ceremonies. Every five years, as *Duoviri Quinquennales*, they were additionally charged with the task of revising property lists and public contracts, and enrolling new members into the *Ordo*. As executive officers they were assisted by two *Aediles*, whose area of responsibility was the maintenance of public buildings, streets and drains, and by two *Quaestores* responsible for local finance. The colonies were additionally centres of the imperial cult, the maintenance and financing of which was largely the responsibility of the *Seviri Augustales* (see chapter 7).

Similar to the colonies in many respects, though of lower status, was the *municipium*, usually a pre-existing settlement within a province taken over by Rome. The one certain instance in Britain, at Verulamium (St. Albans), was in fact founded close to what had once been the capital of the Catuvellauni, and this probably accounts for its status. Like the colonies, the municipium controlled a considerable area of land round about it and mirrored their administration in its most important posts. Unlike Colchester when first founded, though, the inhabitants of the municipium were not necessarily of full citizen status.

The Civitates

While Rome saw urbanisation, the establishment of a life-style typical of the Mediterranean, as a prime necessity in making Britain civilised, the native population followed a far less centralised way of life, which necessitated in consequence a different approach to local government when this was established. The result consisted of *civitates peregrinae*, which converted the old tribal areas into Roman administrative units, or grouped into manageable units what had once been separate tribes but were now regarded as too small to merit a separate existence. The provision of such autonomous *civitates* was not the result of any basic principle, though, but of a desire to shift responsibility for administration onto the local population as soon as was practicable, hence its probable inception under Vespasian when conditions in the south stabilised. Each had its own administrative centre, the civitas capital, easily recognised by its double-barrelled name - Ratae Coritanorum, Ratae of the Coritani (Leicester), or Calleva Atrebatum, Calleva of the Atrebates (Silchester), for instance. Such towns, however, did not become separate entities, but merely formed part of the whole civitas. One result of this was that the legal point of origin for the non-citizen population was their civitas as a whole, whereas for those enrolled in municipia and colonies it was the town that served this purpose. Inside the civitas local administration reflected the system which operated in the colonies, with the exception of *Quaestores* and *Seviri Augustales*, who no longer figure. Undoubtedly in the early years of the province holding office as local magistrates was deemed a source of considerable honour, despite the heavy financial outlay expected of them through the provision of municipal amenities. With time, however, such financial burdens became great enough for evasion of office to rank high among the concerns of the well-to-do and for an element of coercion to be deemed necessary in order to secure holders of office.

Within the area of the civitates we find mention of two other units, the *vicus* and the *pagus*. The first was the smallest unit of self-administration; indeed some civitas capitals had this status, but it was also given to city wards and to civil settlements that grew up around forts, especially those along Hadrian's Wall. In contrast, the *pagus* was a subdivision of the civitas itself, a rural area the administration of which remains obscure. However, since some of the civitates, like that of the Durotriges, were later divided, the *pagus* may have formed the area that could be developed into a civitas in its own right. This may be the origin of the Carvetii, who came to constitute a civitas separate from the Brigantes.

Although the administrations of the civitates were naturally concerned for the most part with local issues, they did also send delegates to the Provincial Council, a body with few powers, and these largely restricted to praising or criticising governors. It was, though, the one body that could air matters on a provincial-wide basis or could raise matters in Rome itself through patrons such as Marcus Vettius Valens in the mid-second century or Gaius Julius Asper in the early decades of the third century. Otherwise its chief function seems to have been maintenance of the province's central imperial cult, itself a costly undertaking.

Changes with time
With time the deficiencies of provincial administration became apparent when Britain became the power base for usurpers like Clodius Albinus in AD 193-7, and then Carausius and Allectus in 287-96. The response of Rome in each case was to divide Britain (see Fig.11), like other such provinces on the continent, into smaller, and

therefore less powerful, units: first into two, *Britannia Inferior* and *Superior*, the former in the north and including both York and Lincoln, the latter in the south but including Chester. In terms of status it is clear that *Superior* with its two legions and consular governor was the more important, compared to *Inferior* with its single legion and governor of only praetorian rank. When in 296 the Caesar Constantius recovered Britain from Allectus, the division was further extended into four elements, *Britannia Prima* and *Britannia Maxima Caesariensis* formed out of *Britannia Superior*, while *Britannia Secunda* and *Britannia Flavia Caesariensis* were formed from *Britannia Inferior*. Additionally, each was now to be governed by a *Praeses* of equestrian rank (though later the Praeses of *Maxima Caesariensis* became consular in status), while the whole of Britain now constituted a Diocese headed by a Vicar or deputy of the western Praetorian Prefect. With time a further division of power was to occur with the separation of military and civil authority. The former passed into the hands of a Duke of the Provinces of Britain and the Count of the Saxon Shore, while civil power remained with the *Praesides* and the Vicar. This multiplication of power at the highest level was matched of course by that in the administration in general, and was further intensified by additional complexities introduced by Diocletian into the realm of finance-generation. This itself was now divided between a process of requisition and taxation proper under a Count of the Sacred Largesses, who collected taxes from both the population as a whole (*res summa*) and from the imperial estates (*res privata*) through his representatives in Britain, the *Rationalis Summarum Britanniarum* and *Rationalis Rei Privatae Per Britannias*, each with his own staff. Under Diocletian and his successors not only did the administration expand, it also became more oppressive as more and more responsibility fell onto the shoulders of the decurions of the *Ordo,* who became personally responsible for the collection of those taxes allotted to them and any shortfall incurred, recruitment to the army and the maintenance of roads. Membership of the *Ordo* had also by now become hereditary, with escape only through promotion to higher status, and what had once been a privilege now became an imposition.

Chapter 6
Towns and the Countryside

There is a vast range of information available for the civilian side of life in Roman Britain and we can only skim the surface of it here. Most of the information for this aspect of the Roman occupation, and for the processes of Romanisation, is archaeological, since the historical sources are more concerned with conquest and politics than daily life. However, Tacitus' cynical view of life in the province is worth including at this point:

> To induce a people, hitherto scattered, uncivilised and therefore prone to fight, to grow pleasurably inured to peace and ease, Agricola gave private encouragement and official assistance to the building of temples, public squares and private mansions. He praised the keen and scolded the slack, and competition to gain honour from him was as effective as compulsion. Furthermore, he trained the sons of the chiefs in the liberal arts and expressed a preference for British natural ability over the trained skill of the Gauls. The result was that in place of distaste for the Latin language came a passion to command it. In the same way our national dress came into favour and the toga was everywhere to be seen. And so the Britons were gradually led on to the amenities that make vice agreeable - arcades, baths and sumptuous banquets. They spoke of such novelties as 'civilisation', when really they were only a feature of enslavement.

(TACITUS, *Agricola*, 21)

As ever, Tacitus presents an extreme view, but the kernel of truth which can be discerned in this passage is that the Britons would not necessarily have objected to being incorporated in a Roman province as long as there were material advantages to be gained from that change. Put simply, the rise in living standards brought by Roman 'civilisation' was more than sufficient to sweeten the bitter pill of conquest. Boudicca's rebellion can be seen as much a protest against rapaciousness on the part of the occupying administration as it was a protest against the occupation itself, and we may recall here the inclusive statement, quoted earlier, that Hadrian's Wall was built to 'separate the Romans from the barbarians'. This shows how as early as the second century the provincials in Britain were considered to be inside the pale. It was a fundamentally important aspect of the Roman empire that it displayed a remarkable tolerance towards, and ability to assimilate, foreign culture. Nowhere was this clearer than in the matter of religion (see chapter 7), but adaptation and assimilation were the key to all aspects of the success of the Roman empire.

The Economy
We have seen in preceding chapters that urbanisation was the basic element in the process of Romanisation of new territory, and Britain was no exception to the rule that inclusion within the Roman empire was consolidated by the establishment of a network of roads and cities. But these cities were economic entities. In order for them to flourish there had to be a secure economic base, and the basis of the economy of Roman Britain therefore has to be the point of origin in any consideration of settlement patterns in the province.

The most fundamental economic change effected by the Romans was in terms of the basic infrastructure. Foremost was the establishment of a currency which was not only stable but also universal. Hitherto, such currency as had existed had been tribally based, and interchange at more than a local level must have been difficult. By the end of the first century Britain also had a very effective network of roads and market centres both of which were prerequisites for effective commerce. Exploitation of mineral resources was swift. Even before the occupation of Britain minerals, notably tin, were being exported from Britain to the Roman sphere of influence on the continent and in the late pre-Roman iron age Britain had also been an exporter of worked products in bronze. The occupying forces wasted no time in exploiting the mineral resources of the island and already during the reign of Claudius the extraction of lead, and its attendant silver, was well under way in the Mendips. By the 70s lead was also being produced in Clwyd. Gold was mined at Dolaucothi in Dyfed and the tin industry in Cornwall was maintained. Iron was worked in the Weald and the Forest of Dean, whilst copper was extracted in north Wales. Mineral rights were taken as the exclusive prerogative of the emperor, and areas of mineral production accordingly became imperial estate. This may help to explain why areas like the southwest of England show up as blanks in Fig.14 which shows the distribution of villas in Roman Britain.

Other productive activities were established which were necessary for internal purposes, and the production of bricks and pots for local consumption was raised to a high level in a remarkably short time after the conquest. Pottery products, particularly fine wares and special goods like the heavy *mortaria* (mortar) used for grinding vegetables and herbs, were traded far and wide throughout the province, whilst tiles and bricks were mainly produced for local consumption.

The major activity in the Roman empire which provided the basis of its economy was, however, that of agriculture (see below). Roman Britain was no exception in this respect and , however advanced and complex the industrial systems in any town were, it would nevertheless have been predominantly dependent on its agricultural hinterland for economic survival. The positioning of cities in the newly conquered province was driven, therefore, largely by the economic consideration of finding suitable locations for market centres that had good access to the developing road system. It is a mark of the confidence which prevailed in the early empire that not much account seems to have been taken of considerations of defence in locating urban centres, though it has to be noted that there was military advantage for the occupying forces in the shift of centres of population from defensible upland sites to more accessible lowland positions.

Towns and Cities

The level of urban prosperity or decline was a major indicator of the health of the Roman empire at any point in its history, and was as valid an indicator for Britain as for any other province even though Britain was never completely urbanised. As we have seen in the preceding chapter, there was a variety of types of urban settlement in Britain ranging from the *colony* with its full citizen body, often starting with a core of retired legionaries, through *municipia* to the various types of *civitas*. Colonies are few in Britain, and in many ways they were independent units standing outside the day-to-day administrative systems of the province. Cities such as London which technically had lower constitutional status were nevertheless the main mercantile centres of the province, whilst the civitas capitals were the Roman equivalent of county towns where assizes and other important gatherings were held. At the bottom end of the urban scale were the small roadside settlements which grew up throughout the province and the *vici* which arose beside military centres, especially in northern England, where the full processes of urbanisation were never completed.

Cities in Roman Britain were not large by modern standards, and the colonies were not the largest among the Roman cities in the province. The extent of Roman London is reckoned at about 133 hectares, and the next largest city, Cirencester, at about 100 hectares in extent. By comparison Colchester, largest of the colonies, covered only about 44 hectares. The relative sizes can be gauged from Fig.12 in which plans showing the extent of London and Colchester are juxtaposed. At the bottom of the scale were very insubstantial urban centres such as Brough-on-Humber which had an area of just 5 hectares. Larger cities acted as administrative centres for their regions and had the necessary public buildings to serve these purposes. Smaller towns had no such function. There is a noticeable difference between the well planned and organised major towns and the smaller urban centres like Kenchester in Herefordshire and Wall (Letocetum) in Leicestershire where ribbon development along Roman roads developed to the point at which it was appropriate to enclose the settlement with walls, but no concerted grid plan was possible.

The population of Roman Britain is variously estimated at totals between two and six million, with the latter seeming more likely as continuing discoveries are made, especially through the medium of aerial photography. It is impossible to calculate what proportion of the population would have been resident in towns. But, given the great significance of agriculture as the main industry of Roman Britain, it is likely that the majority of the population lived in the countryside, whilst a very substantial proportion of the province's wealth would have existed in the towns, at least during the first and second centuries. The creation of a network of towns is one of the most enduring aspects of the Roman achievement, and the success of the sites chosen can be seen from the fact

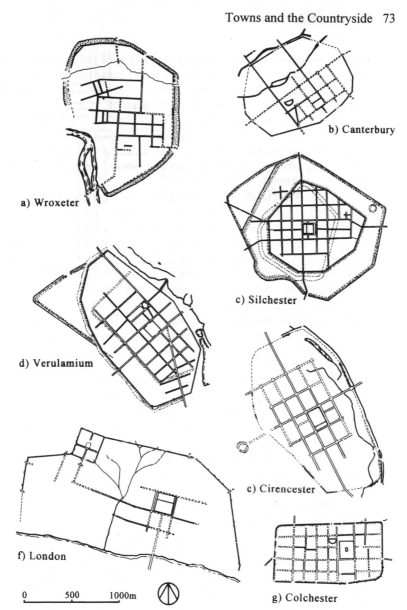

a) Wroxeter

b) Canterbury

c) Silchester

d) Verulamium

e) Cirencester

f) London

g) Colchester

0 500 1000m

Fig.12 Principal towns of Roman Britain (after Collingwood and Richmond).

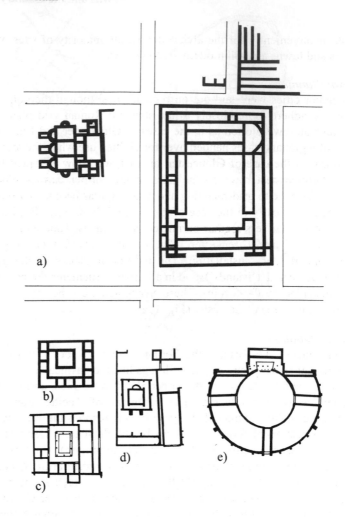

Fig. 13   Building types in towns (after Wacher 1995).
a) Central insulae of Leicester showing Jewry Wall Baths
complex and Forum-Basilica complex ; b) Macellum at
Wroxeter; c) Courtyard house at Caerwent; d) Temple and
adjoining shop at Caerwent; e) Theatre at St. Albans.

that, inconveniently for the archaeologist, the majority of sites of Roman cities and towns are still modern urban centres.

Town Planning

All major cities were laid out on regular lines, though the colonies were likely to adhere more closely to the standard Roman grid plan, not least because they were often as in the cases of Gloucester and Lincoln on the sites of legionary bases handed over for civilian use when the army moved forward. In the case of Gloucester, at least, we know that private houses were built in neat rows on the lines of the former barrack-blocks. The strict adherence to grid-planning and a rectangular perimeter for a *colonia* can be seen clearly in the case of the plan of Colchester (Fig.12g). Other cities which had less regular perimeters nevertheless adopted the grid plan especially if like Cirencester (Fig.12e) they owed their origins to a preceding military installation. The individual blocks of the grid were known as *insulae* ('islands'), and in all urban settlements the central *insula* was occupied by the forum. These arrangments can be seen very clearly in the central area of Leicester (Fig. 13a).

Public Buildings

In provinces like Britain the forum tended to be a fairly uniform rectangular space where public buildings like the basilica, used for judicial purposes, and the temple of the imperial cult were sited, and business and commerce were conducted. The comment of Tacitus quoted at the beginning of this chapter that Agricola was responsible for encouraging the construction of fora is borne out by the dedicatory inscription of the forum in the *municipium* of St. Albans (Verulamium) which was erected in AD 79 and contains Agricola's name. The forum at St. Albans was a very grand affair measuring 94 by 62 metres: ranged round this forum behind a colonnaded walkway were a basilica, a *curia*, or Council house, and two temples. Most fora were rather less grand, often following the pattern adopted at Silchester where the forum consisted of a space measuring 43 by 39 metres, with a colonnade and shops on three sides and the west side occupied by the basilical hall. Although no forum and basilica remains intact, parts of these buildings are among the most substantial non-military relics of Roman Britain, and the Mint Wall at Lincoln serves very well to convey a real sense of the monumentality of these Roman urban centres.

As well as the monumental complexes with forum and basilica which served the administrative needs of the Roman town, it is to be expected that most would have had a permanent market hall (*macellum*) such as has been found at Leicester, St. Albans and Wroxeter (Fig. 13b). These buildings consisted of runs of shops ranged round the sides of courtyards with space for temporary stalls at the centre. Alterations to the *macellum* at St. Albans, which was equipped with a large raised platform, may have been designed to create the space for a *ponderarium* (public weights and measures office).

In addition to countless statues of emperors and imperial and civic dignitaries, some cities are known to have had grandiose public monuments. There was a magnificent four-way arch (*tetrapylum*) at Richborough (Rutupiae) on the Kent coast. This was constructed in AD 80-90 and marked the main entry to the province, being built presumably to celebrate the point at which the process of conquest was complete. There were at least three triumphal arches at St. Albans. All stood on the line of Watling Street, with two at the main gateways of the city and another near the theatre. Parts of a monumental column dedicated to Jupiter Optimus Maximus by the fourth century governor of *Britannia Prima* can be seen in the Cirencester Museum.

Other important public buildings may be divided into those with a social function (i.e. baths, theatres and amphitheatres), those with a religious function (i.e. temples) and those structures, notably aqueducts and sewers, which provided public services. All are known in Roman Britain, but whilst bath-houses and temples were universally present, buildings concerned with entertainment are less common.

Temples

Religion in Roman Britain is considered separately in chapter 7. Here it must suffice to note the diversity of architectural types from the simple square so-called Romano-Celtic temple which may be seen, as foundations at least, in the remains of the urban settlement at Caerwent (Fig. 13d), through to the grand precinct and temple of the imperial and provincial cult at Colchester which was the meeting place of the annual provincial assembly and, as such, an architectural focus for provincial unity. As in other aspects of Romanisation the essentially tolerant attitude to Celtic religion, reflected in the survival of native forms of temple, is an important factor contributing to the successful 'civilisation' of the province. The Romano-Celtic type of temple was inherited from the pre-Roman period and consisted of a square structure surrounded by a verandah and containing a high central shrine lit by clerestory windows. The vast temple of Claudius at Colchester and the temple of Sulis-Minerva at Bath on the other hand were both very Classical in form, standing on high platforms (*podia*) with columnar façades supporting decorated pediments. Again, there is considerable variety in terms of scale, and it should not be forgotten that the most common type of religious structure was the simple rectangular shrine such as the temple of Antenociticus which may be seen between the vallum and Hadrian's Wall at Benwell in western Newcastle upon Tyne.

Theatres
The remains of only one theatre, that at St. Albans (Fig. 13e), can be seen above ground today, but we know that there were theatres at Brough-on-Humber, Canterbury, Colchester and Gosbecks Farm near Colchester. Roman theatres were normally D-shaped structures, but the theatre at St. Albans combined an almost circular arena with a stage building and it seems that this theatre could have been used for the kinds of display normally shown in amphitheatres. These were generally more popular than theatres in the western provinces, and Roman Britain seems to have been no exception to this generalisation. As well as the military amphitheatres found near the legionary fortresses of Caerleon and Chester, remains of amphitheatres may be seen at Aldborough, Carmarthen, Chichester, Cirencester, Dorchester (Maumbury Rings, a converted neolithic henge) and Silchester. We know too from excavation that there were late amphitheatres at Caerwent and Richborough. All these amphitheatres consisted of earthen banks rather than monumental stone constructions but were no less functional for that. These structures would have accommodated large numbers watching gladiatorial contests, animal displays and public executions, or attending public meetings.

Bath-houses
Bath-houses were an essential element in Roman life. Like temples, they ranged from the modest to the monumental, and as a consequence of their vital social function they could often become almost as important for the

conduct of law, administration and above all business and commerce as the forum and basilica. The basic principles which directed the planning of bath-houses applied to all baths, small or large, since all bath-houses operated a system in which the bathers moved from room to room. Most commonly the bath-house resembled its successor, the Turkish baths, and contained three main bathing rooms each at a different temperature. After undressing in the *apodyterium* (changing-room) the bather would proceed to the *frigidarium* (cold room) which would be heated only slightly, if at all, and would contain a cold plunge-bath. The next room was the *tepidarium* (warm room). Then the bather entered the *caldarium* (hot room), a steamy room heated to a temperature which caused the bathers to sweat and contained a very hot plunge bath normally positioned very close to, or directly on top of, the furnaces. After a spell in the hot plunge-bath the bather returned backwards through the system to the cold plunge. Some bath-houses had the further refinements of a *laconicum* (hot dry room) and a *palaestra* (exercise yard).

Smaller urban bath-houses are indistinguishable from the bath-houses which were attached to forts. Thus the public baths at Silchester consist of a simple row of spaces and rooms providing a palaestra and *apodyterium*, and the rooms for the three stages of the bathing process, with a *laconicum* attached to the side of the *tepidarium*. The whole complex is about 48 metres long, with the bathing rooms occupying a total length of 20 metres. In terms of plan and size the baths at Silchester compare very closely with the military bath-house of the auxiliary fort at Hardknot in Cumbria. The massive scale of some the civic bath-houses can be gauged from the Old Work at Wroxeter which still stands eight metres high: here the whole complex was 122 metres long with the bathing rooms taking up 46 metres. But the plan is in essence nothing more than a magnified version of the plan of the Silchester bath-house, differing only in having a pair of *apodyteria* with attached *laconica*. Another grand civic bath-house, the Jewry Wall complex at Leicester, had parallel sets of bathing chambers. This may have allowed for simultaneous male and female bathing, though normally provision for this was made by arranging rotas and controlling the times and days of admission. The massive Jewry Wall itself was originally the dividing wall between the exercise hall and the changing room.

All the bath-houses mentioned so far were, of course, eclipsed by the enormous bath complex at Bath. This was a special case, for the baths exploited the sacred hot springs which were the reason for the foundation of Aquae Sulis ('waters of Sulis') in the first place, and which attracted visitors for healing purposes from throughout the province and even from the continent. Another context in which bath-houses are found is that of the large courtyard buildings which have been found immediately inside the gateways of Silchester and Caerwent. These buildings were probably inns which provided small bath-houses as part of their services for travellers.

Military baths were often enough placed near convenient natural water supplies. When the site of the fort at Corbridge moved from the Red House, now under the Corbridge by-pass, to the site of the present town, the bath-house remained beside the stream which was the cause of its original location.

For baths to flourish in an urban context, however, it was necessary to provide adequate water supplies through artificial channels. In the case of the colonies the citizens would have benefited from the efforts of the skilled military engineers who produced, for instance, the elaborate covered and pressurised aqueduct system that drove water uphill through concrete-sheathed pipes into Lincoln. The head of the supply system inside the city was probably a large pressurised cistern (*castellum aquae*) that may have stood on a heavy platform which has been found against the north wall of the colony. The water was distributed round the city through lead pipes. Access was also provided at fountain-houses where open tanks — like the octagonal basin which was found in the lower city at Lincoln — were filled for people to collect water in containers. Lincoln was additionally provided with a grid of built underground sewers to remove foul and storm waters. The complex aqueduct and drainage system known at Lincoln, though not uncommon in imperial terms, is exceptional in Roman Britain. Most cities were supplied by open aqueduct systems where water ran into the city in leats such as the Raw Dykes earthwork which can be seen coming into Leicester from the south. Such leats are known to have supplied water to Caerwent, Caistor-by-Norwich, Cirencester, Dorchester, St. Albans, Silchester and Wroxeter.

Houses

As in modern towns, the most common buildings of all were houses, shops and small business premises. Frequently these were combined in long strip buildings with a short end containing a retail shop or workshop on the street frontage. In some cases, as has been seen above, the blocks occupied by military barrack units were taken over to provide the sites of what were in effect terraces of domestic buildings with integral shops and workshops. Rows of such buildings doubtless existed in all the towns of Roman Britain. They have been detected at Caerwent, St. Albans, Wroxeter, and also in the *vicus* which was set up outside the fort at Housesteads on Hadrian's Wall. Sometimes the strip-houses were extended by the addition of extra rooms at the back or side of the buildings. Richer citizens had town houses which resembled both the courtyard houses of the Mediterranean and the quarters occupied by officers in the military forts. In these houses rooms occupied three or sometimes four sides of the courtyard and parts of the buildings were heated by hypocaust systems. Such houses have been found at at Caerwent (Fig. 13c), Cirencester and Leicester. Fragments of decoration excavated from these buildings provide evidence for elaborately painted walls to complement the mosaic floors which have been found at the sites of most of the towns of Roman Britain. In effect, the variety of forms of town house bears a strong resemblance to the range of types of domestic buildings found on the villa estates which are considered below.

It is important to note that the distinction between town and country could be extremely blurred since often enough town houses stood in large parcels of land which served as urban smallholdings inside the walls of Roman cities. Several of the buildings at Silchester were probably the houses of urban farms and the presence of such farms has also been suggested at St. Albans and Wroxeter. An early fourth century building complex inside Cirencester had a house with at least nine rooms, some with mosaic floors and painted walls, which formed part of an enclosure with three barns. The only feature apart from its location inside a city which distinguishes this complex from its rural equivalent, the villa, is the absence of a bath-house. Since attendance at the public bath-house was a common method of meeting business associates in town, we may assume that the rich owner of the property at Cirencester did not see a private bath-house as a necessary feature on his urban farm.

Urban Defences

It was noted above that the locations of cities in Roman Britain were determined by economic and trading considerations rather than defence. However, almost all urban centres were equipped with defences and, as conditions became less secure, these defences were often strengthened so that now the most common and impressive remains of the urban centres of Roman Britain are their walls. As an indicator of urban prosperity or decline it is always of interest to observe how the walls of cities throughout the Roman empire expand and contract in terms of area and thickness throughout time. The changes in urban defence systems also reflect the changes in thinking which are clear from the defences of Roman forts. These, as we have seen, develop from the lighter defences of the first century turf and timber forts, which were essentially offensive establishments, through to the heavily defended forts of the Saxon Shore. The walls of Silchester have three phases which display the expansion of the city and its subsequent contraction. On the other hand the well-preserved walls of London and Caerwent show particularly clearly how projecting artillery bastions were added in the fourth century to what were already heavily defensive fortifications erected during the third. The evidence of the city walls of Roman Britain, in other words, is eloquent testimony to the replacement of early confidence and expansionism with subsequent contraction and general feelings of insecurity.

The colonies of Gloucester and Lincoln both had sets of defences by the early second century. The early defences of the colonies consisted of earthen banks about 1.5 metres thick, with internal stone towers which apparently simply occupied the previously existing lines of the walls of the legionary fortresses and were faced with stone revetments. The elaboration of these defences illustrates the growing perception in the province of Roman Britain that ever stronger defences were necessary since in due course they were thickened, wholly replaced in stone and raised in height. The walls of London first erected around AD 200 are interesting for their inclusion, on the northwest side, of the defences of the Cripplegate fort which was created about 100 years earlier for the garrison of the city. Significant portions of the city wall survive to heights approaching 5 metres showing it was constructed from flint rubble and mortar faced by small squared stones and provided with horizontal tile bonding courses at regular intervals of about a metre. The London wall stands on a heavy foundation projecting forward in front of the curtain which itself varies between 2.1 and 2.8 metres in thickness. Behind this formidable stone and concrete wall was a heavy earthen bank about 4.25 metres thick. In the fourth century, perhaps in the 340s, London in common with other cities in Roman Britain further strengthened its defences by the addition of forward-projecting bastions strong enough to support artillery devices. These bastions were constructed from solid stone and contained much material re-used from Roman buildings and extracted from the monuments in the surrounding cemeteries. The practice of despoiling funerary monuments to provide building materials for defences is known from other parts of the empire. The most famous example are the magnificent monuments incorporated in the walls of Trier in Germany, though it can be argued that the process occurred in Britain slightly later than was the case on the continent. This is one of the factors indicating that whilst retrenchment was undoubtedly occurring in Britain in the third century the island was relatively protected from the problems rife on the continent.

Urban Decline

Other pieces of evidence show that there was significant urban decline by the fourth century. The basilica of the forum of Silchester was sub-divided in the late third century into small units which were used for metal processing. The great public baths and exercise court at Wroxeter ceased to be maintained and was abandoned by about 300. The forum and basilica at Leicester were destroyed by fire in the early fourth century and never rebuilt. These are poignant indicators of urban malaise. Contemporary evidence from the villas and country estates flourishing in Britain in the early fourth century shows that at that time wealth was flowing from town to country. The towns were degenerating into poorly maintained market centres and increasingly, as trade declined, the country estates were forced to become self-sufficient, inward-looking, units with less and less contact with the declining urban centres. In this way the stage was set for the patterns of land-holding which were to prevail in the middle ages. It is to the villas and the countryside that we must now turn after a brief consideration of the agricultural developments which fuelled the growth of both towns and country estates in Roman Britain.

Agriculture

Although trade and industry were important, agriculture was the main productive activity in the Roman empire, and was so in Britain, since the cities which transformed social patterns were all dependent on their agricultural hinterlands to survive. The Romans brought with them new crops and tools, but the agricultural revolution which led to greatly increased levels of agricultural production was well under way before the conquest. Even so, given the need to feed the army of occupation, which at first must have had to import significant quantities of food stuffs, as well as the newly established towns and cities, there was urgent need to develop the agricultural economy of Britain immediately after the conquest. The great change during the Roman occupation was in terms of the extent and type of land which could be turned to arable use. This change was swiftest and most lasting in the southern and central parts of England where the villa system was to take strongest root. In part the development of agriculture in Britain was made possible by greater availability of good tools: in the Roman period iron was in better supply, and ordinary farmers accordingly gained access to iron-shod spades and ploughs as well as to steel axes. All these were sharper, more durable and better able to deal, for instance, with the heavy clay soils of the Midlands. Even the sickle was improved by the addition of a better handle which improved its balance and swing. But the most significant improvements were to the plough. This gained both its horizontal-bladed iron ploughshare and the addition of the coulter board which meant that it now turned the soil over rather than merely cutting a slit through it. It was during the Roman occupation that furrows appeared for the first time in British fields. Fields were also improved by better knowledge of methods of drainage and the construction of wells. As a consequence of these simple technological advances, woodland was more easily cleared and marshland more easily drained. The effect was to cause significant alteration to the long-static British landscape and a shift from short term subsistence to stable surplus in agricultural terms.

Most farming in Iron Age and Roman Britain was mixed (i.e. a combination of arable and pastoral). Owing to the lack of winter fodder Iron age farmers had been obliged to conduct annual culls of their herds and flocks. Consequently they had been unable to build up animal stocks as only small numbers of breeding animals could be fed through the winter months. Larger herds and flocks meant that there could be surpluses of dairy products and wool; and manufactured items made from woollen materials, notably the *Birrus Britannicus* — a sort of thick duffel coat — were significant exports during the third and fourth centuries.

There were changes, too, in terms of crops. Traditionally the cereals grown in Britain had been barley and emmer wheat. Both are resistant to damp and mould and therefore suitable for the British climate, but neither grain produces bread flour. Emmer has the further disadvantage that though it stores well its husks are so hard that the grain has to be toasted before it can be winnowed and milled. The Romans encouraged the growth of spelt, which could be sown during winter and produced a much finer flour than would previously have been available. Rye, oats and flax were also encouraged. Granaries which were raised above ground and barns with adequate drains and ventilation allowed for the storage of surplus arable production. The Roman period saw the introduction of a range of root crops — including turnips, carrots and parsnips — new varieties of bean, peas, celery, and cabbage. Some of these, too, were winter crops which helped to resolve the problem of keeping flocks and herds fed throughout the year.

Even field systems changed. The traditional Celtic field was a roughly square shape which suffered from developing headlands where the soil moved by the plough built up, gradually reducing the cultivable area. Roman fields were of rectangular plan, commonly about 80 metres long and 30 metres wide and with smaller headlands. Both types of field co-existed in Roman Britain, with the richer villa estates tending to have the longer and thinner Roman type of field. It is very difficult to estimate size of estate or level of agricultural activity. However, from evidence such as the excavation of the byre in the villa at Pitney, which is thought to have had about 150 hectares of arable land when the byre held six or seven pairs of oxen, we may assume that a pair of oxen was needed for about 23 hectares of arable land. Medieval records suggest a ration of one pair of oxen to 20 hectares. One of the most profound effects of the Roman occupation was the development of the landscape for more intensive agricultural purposes. This development of the agricultural economy was the context in which the cities and villas operated.

Villas and Country Estates

The term 'villa' is problematic. In modern accounts the word is often used to describe the buildings which formed the handsome residences of the more wealthy country estates of Roman Britain, and so it will have to be used here. But in fact to a Roman the word simply meant 'a farm' and as such it should really be applied to the whole estate including any buildings, however modest and unlovely, that estate contained.

There is the further problem of who owned and lived in these villas. Apart from exceptional cases like the grand fourth century courtyard villa at Woodchester in Gloucestershire which may have been constructed for an imperial official, their owners would normally have been wealthy Romano-British, that is to say not Romans as such but members of the upper classes of native society who had become thoroughly Romanised. Viewed in this way it is possible to understand the processes by which the farm-house at Lockleys (Fig. 15) developed from a simple Belgic hut into a much more complicated and impressive winged corridor 'villa'. Whilst one need not assume continuity of ownership of the estate within one family (though that is not precluded), it is necessary to assume continuity of the land-owning classes of British society. Their inclusion in the upper strata of Romano-British society was a necessary condition for the securing of the process of Romanisation. The presence in the grand villas of heating systems, mosaics and wall paintings shows how the Romano-British upper classes came to enjoy the benefits of Roman civilisation. Introduced to such privileges, they would have fought as strongly as any to preserve and defend their province. Such people, too, who would have been the aristocrats of pre-Roman Britain, would now have served as its councillors and magistrates. Occasionally, as in the case of the villa at Chedworth, there are two sets of domestic apartments. The possibility exists that the villa may have seen multiple occupancy by more than one family or by more than one generation of the same family.

Villas, then, were commonly the country houses of rich families which also had expensive town houses. Like the country seats of landowners in England in the 18th and 19th centuries, the villas would have been used for summer and weekend entertainment of social peers and business associates. In villas the luxuries of town were brought to the country where tired city businessmen could combine country pursuits like hunting with the traditional pastime of a session in the bath-house. The domestic quarters of the villa at Great Witcombe in Gloucestershire, barely a stone's throw from Gloucester itself, appear to be on the minimalist side, but the house has a long verandah with a fine view and a fine dining room (*triclinium*) as well as an extensive bath-suite. In other words the needs of entertainment are fully catered for, though one wonders whether the establishment was really meant to be lived in for lengthy periods. The villa at Great Witcombe does, however, have extensive servants' quarters and it is clear that the practical needs of the farm were well provided for. Presumably the farm at Great Witcombe, like so many others in the Roman empire, could be run at a handsome profit by a bailiff employed by a landowner who would not have needed to maintain regular personal oversight of the farming activities. Villas, in other words, had two functions: one was the grand business of entertainment and recreation for the Romano-British upper classes, the other was as productive farming units. The former function explains the luxurious reception rooms and bath-houses. Evidence for the latter consists of barns, stables, mills and corn-dryers, and all the other mundane structures associated with the production of food. However, it is doubtful whether all villas performed both functions.

Since we cannot establish the size of the estates, it is impossible to prove that some fine country houses were built simply for the occasional recreation of the upper classes. Yet there are sites where only the most functional houses are found and it seems reasonable to suppose in these cases that the estates were perhaps run by bailiffs with the landowner rarely if ever making an appearance. The villa at Hambleden in Buckinghamshire had a huge capacity for drying corn but was apparently lacking in barns and granaries. To explain this phenomenon it has been argued that the estate may have been state property, used for the production of corn to feed the armies active in the northern parts of the province. The argument derives some support from the discovery at Hambleden of 70 bronze pens which could have been used by the government clerks who would have been needed to document the production and distribution of the corn. Clearly, then, the villa at Hambleden was predominantly an economic concern. We can be certain that it was run by slave labour from the grim evidence of no less than 97 infant burials in the farmyard area in front of the villa and its outbuildings. These babies were the unfortunate products of illicit unions between members of the labour force of an agricultural unit which must have been run like a prison camp.

The living conditions of the permanent residents of the villas represent the down side of this hitherto opulent picture since many of those who lived on the villa estates would have been slaves or else tenant-farmers bound as virtual serfs in debt-bondage to the landowners. The system needed slaves for full economic efficiency though this left smallholders and tenants in very weak positions as they were unable to generate saleable produce in sufficient quantities to enable them to compete in the open market. These lower classes of villa society would have had to live in much inferior accommodation, and it is presumably these people who occupied the cottages (*casae*) that continued to be constructed right through to the end of the use of the villas. Meanwhile the so-called 'aisled barns' (Fig. 16a and 16b), another simple type of house found on the villa estates, were either bailiffs' houses or, more likely, used as communal quarters for slaves. Some of the aisled structures, as can be seen in the building at Landwade in Suffolk, display signs of internal divisions which could have provided privacy for bailiffs living under the same roof as their work-force. Often enough, as at Llantwit Major in mid Glamorgan, an aisled barn was built beside a grander villa suggesting a degree of social differentiation between the landowner and his employees and slaves. The case of Llantwit Major is interesting since in the last years of occupation of the villa the main house and the bath-suite were abandoned, but the aisled barn continued in use indicating presumably that though the landowner had no further interest in occupying his villa the estate continued as a productive agricultural unit.

The distribution of villas (Fig. 14) is significant. It reflects the distribution of towns in Roman Britain and also, as has been seen, the presence of imperial estates where there were significant mineral resources or where, as in the case of the lands round the Wash, productive arable land may have been inherited by the emperor from the tribal lands of the Iceni or drained by imperial engineers. The majority of villas are concentrated on the south side of, or in the immediate vicinity of, the Fosse Way. This fact has been used to defend the idea that the Fosse Way should be seen as some sort of early frontier. However, it is safer to see this evidence as showing that the villa system was part of the process of Romanisation which was more fully effected in those parts of the province

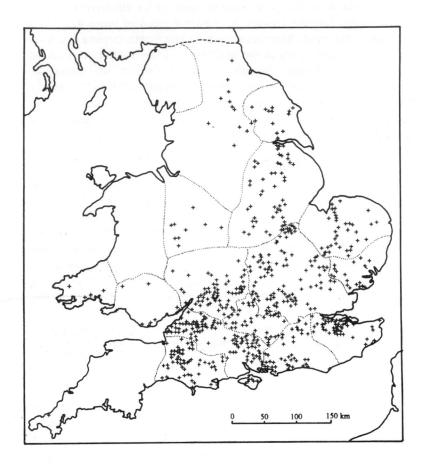

Fig. 14   Distribution of Roman villas known in Britain in relation to the *civitates* (after Rivet).

first to be conquered and which contained the richest farming land. Pockets of villas exist, for instance, in south Wales, Yorkshire and Humberside, but it is clear that much of western and northern Britain continued the farming practices current before the Roman occupation. The farming settlements of Roman Brigantia differed only in the matter of available artefacts from the farming settlements of the Brigantes in the late pre-Roman Iron Age. Villas, in other words, were part of the process of handing the province over to civilian control. Like cities, they are absent from those parts of the province which remained in military hands.

As the cities and towns went into decline in the third and fourth centuries the villas seem to have thrived, and it is worth pausing to note that there are signs of villas emerging as coherent social units in their own right, acting somewhat like the manor houses of the middle ages. There is considerable evidence for the practice of Christianity in the fourth century villas even though the word *paganus* (countryman) has given us our word pagan. In the case of the villa at Lullingstone in Kent, the presence of Christianity cannot be doubted since the famous wall paintings which can be now be seen in the British Museum show the Chi-Rho symbol of Christ as well as Christian orant (praying) figures. It is also interesting to observe that the Christian apartments were separated from the rest of the villa, allowing for speculation that they may have been accessible to the local community as a church.

The houses on the estates deserve some consideration in their own right since their development shows how Britain was very much a part of the Roman empire as a whole, following the fashions which prevailed in other provinces and perhaps even, in the fourth century, influencing fashion in other provinces. There has been a tendency to assume a model of continuous development of villa plans, since it is possible to trace the process from the simple *casa* type villa with a row of rooms through to the elaborate courtyard villas of the fourth century (see Fig. 16). We have observed above however, that the simple forms existed throughout the history of Roman Britain and that they often co-existed with more elaborate forms on the same estates.

The villa at Lockleys (Fig. 15), near Welwyn in Hertfordshire, demonstrates the first stages of the architectural development of the villa quite clearly. The first structure on the site was a simple native round house (Fig. 15a). In the first decades of the Roman occupation this was

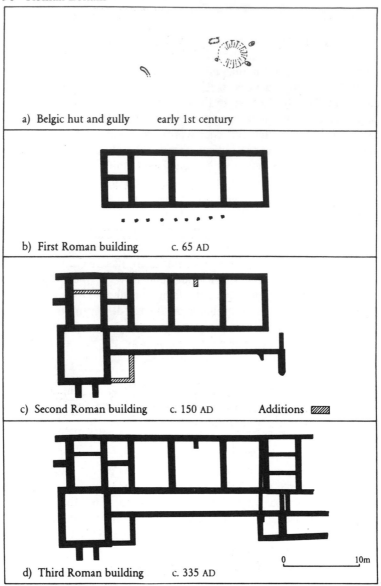

a) Belgic hut and gully   early 1st century

b) First Roman building   c. 65 AD

c) Second Roman building   c. 150 AD   Additions

d) Third Roman building   c. 335 AD

0   10m

Fig. 15   Development of Lockleys Villa (Hertfordshire).

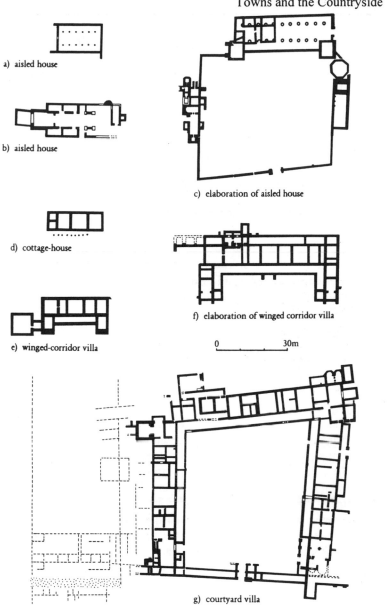

a) aisled house

b) aisled house

c) elaboration of aisled house

d) cottage-house

e) winged-corridor villa

f) elaboration of winged corridor villa

0 _____ 30m

g) courtyard villa

Fig. 16   Comparative plans of types of Roman villas.

replaced by a row house or *casa*, a simple rectangular building with a line of rooms in front of which was a verandah (Fig. 15b). By the middle of the second century the verandah had been replaced by a more substantial corridor and a new wing was added at one end of the building (Fig. 15c). By the middle of the fourth century a further wing was added at the other end of the building, completing its transformation into a 'winged-corridor villa' (Fig. 15d). At all stages in the process the plan of the original suite of rooms from the first Romano-British phase was preserved.

The complete range of villa types is represented in Fig. 16. The simple cottage type is again represented by the early phase of Lockleys (Fig. 16d). It can now be compared with the plans of a simple and an elaborated winged-corridor villa (Fig. 16e and 16f). The logical end of this process is represented here by the villa at North Leigh in Oxfordshire (Fig. 16g) which has a very elaborate plan consisting of buildings ranged round all four sides of a large courtyard. The winged-corridor type of villa became popular in the second century, and was increasingly elaborated until the fourth century saw the full introduction of the courtyard type. The large courtyard villas are untypical in their lavish appointments but still maintained the farming functions of the villa. North Leigh had its farm buildings, and the villa at Chedworth actually had a double courtyard: a fact which has led to the suggestion that the inner courtyard was used as an ornamental garden, whilst the outer one served as the farmyard. That the courtyards were used as farmyards is the logical conclusion which can be drawn from the fact that they were sometimes attached to aisled barns, as happened at Stroud in Gloucestershire (Fig. 16c).

There seems to have been no particular moment which can be said to have marked the end of the villas of Roman Britain. They were flourishing during the first quarter of the fourth century but went into decline thereafter. Even though the comfortable arrangements which were created for the Romano-British aristocracy could not be maintained, and though some villas were abandoned, it is clear that the sites of other villas were occupied into the period beyond the formal end of the Roman occupation of Britain. A pattern which may have been representative of the fate of many of the villas may be seen at Gadebridge Park near Hemel Hempstead in Hertfordshire. Here a winged-corridor house had developed a courtyard by the fourth century. In the fifth century the house and the bath-suite were demolished and their site was taken over for animal pens.

In place of the grand house of the former establishment there was a simple two-roomed cottage. In other words, the lands of the estate continued to be farmed, but there was no longer any need for elaborate living quarters. Gadebridge Park was presumably not the only villa to end with a whimper.

Chapter 7
Religion

The cults of the native Celts

The religions of Celtic Britain, no less than those of Celtic Europe, were centred first and foremost upon nature. The concentration of dedications found in rivers and bogs, streams, groves and wells, for instance, points clearly to the sacredness of such geographical features in the mind of Celtic man. In consequence, many gods were of a distinctly localised nature, like Coventina with her sacred well at Carrawburgh on Hadrian's Wall. An alternative focus for veneration was the animal kingdom, where strength, speed and migration may have suggested powers beyond those natural to man, and hence acted as a source of both wonder and inspiration. In other cases the human head itself was regarded as an object of particular potency: hence the description by Strabo (IV,4,4-5) of head-hunting among the ancient Celts of Gaul and the occurrence in parts of Britain of isolated stone heads. Yet, apart from identifying sacred locations, or associating a name with a god, or gaining some understanding of a god's function from the objects dedicated to him, there is often little more we can say of Celtic religion itself since there are no native literary records to guide us. Instead, what literature has come down to us is entirely the product of Classical writers who were themselves often fumbling to make sense of what they saw or heard. For this reason Caesar at *Gallic War* VI 17 claimed the Gauls worshipped Mercury most of all; not that the statement was true, simply that what he perceived as the supreme god of the Gauls had some affinity with the Roman god. This we see most graphically illustrated in the Roman practice of *interpretatio Romana*, the attempted equation of a Celtic divinity with a Classical counterpart based upon some shared characteristic. The results are fusions such as Sulis Minerva, the one presiding over the hot spring at Bath, the other the Roman goddess of crafts. Similarly, a god worshipped for his martial character, such as Cocidius or Belatucadrus, would inevitably be equated with Mars, while one who stalked the wilderness that still covered much of Britain - like the horned god Cernunnos, or Vinotonus on Scargill Moor near Bowes - would be thought of as a Silvanus figure, the Roman equivalent of the

Greek Pan. Such combining of Roman and native gods in fact was a useful element of policy, suggesting to the native population a point of contact between themselves and their Roman masters, part of the gradual process of Romanisation. The flexibility of a god's functions in both Roman and Celtic pantheons also lent itself to a wide spectrum of possible equation. Cocidius, for instance, though equated at times with Mars, is also found identified with Silvanus, suggesting a rustic as well as a martial aspect.

In addition to the natural features already mentioned there were two other elements of significance for Celtic religion. The first consisted of sacred groves where rites were performed: oak trees in particular seem to have been of special interest. The other took the form of enclosures, at times incorporating a hut that served for a temple, as on Hayling Island in Hampshire. It is clear from the spread of sacrificial remains in such places, however, that it was the precinct itself, with perhaps some associated feature like a spring, well or tree, that was important, not the building. With time Britain below the Severn-Wash line saw the development of such sites into typical Romano-Celtic temples: small square edifices within a square walled precinct, which at times became further developed, as at Harlow, by the addition of extra rooms and an altar in front of the temple itself. For in the Roman mind the temple was not a place for congregational worship but the place where the cult image was housed: hence the small size of such structures.

While the Celtic gods seem not to have inspired much detailed interest in the minds of Classical writers, the Celtic habit of human sacrifice, which was associated with the Druids, proved a perennial source of fascination. Not that human sacrifice need have been at all frequent to judge from the proportion of bones from sheep, goats, cattle and horses found at holy places compared to the occasional finds of human remains. That it existed at all and that the Druids who performed it were supposedly centred upon Britain was enough to draw attention to the island. Whether the Druids themselves were actually priests of the native cults or something quite separate is equally vague. Classical writers often refer to them in terms that equate them with arbitrators, judges, interpreters of omens and philosophers who propounded the transmigration of souls. Other characteristics noted include their use of mistletoe, but first and foremost it was their association with the grisly events of human sacrifice that attracted Roman interest. How prevalent the Druids were in Britain on the other hand is impossible to tell. Most detailed accounts relate to the continent, not Britain, and to the pre-Claudian period. In his narrative of the 55 and 54 BC invasions, for instance, Caesar does not mention coming across them, yet elsewhere in his Commentary he states clearly that Druidism originated in Britain and it was there that Gallic Druids went for higher instruction. Despite this, Tacitus' version of Paulinus' invasion of Anglesey in AD 60 suggests that the very novelty of seeing Druids was one of the factors which caused the Roman troops to halt in their tracks.

The Roman imports

The invasion of AD 43 laid Britain open not only to the enforced influence of Roman administration and technology in all its aspects, but also to the religious cults of the whole empire, both official and personal. With the massive influx of citizens, the greatest proportion of whom in the early years were the soldiers serving in the legions, came the gods of Rome itself, imported as an act of policy, part of the Roman presence. Accompanying the auxiliary troops came the local gods of the provinces from which they were drawn. On a more personal level the opening up of Britain also saw an influx of civilians, speculators and traders who often brought with them the more esoteric cults of the east. Nor indeed was the army itself immune to the influence of such divinities. Soldiers and officials who had served in far-flung provinces were frequently attracted to the gods they found there, and on their move to Britain brought their adopted cults with them, as the many dedications to such gods testify. In the Roman mind it mattered little that an individual might adopt a new faith, so long as that adoption did not involve the rejection of other gods. As pragmatists the Romans were unconcerned as to how many divinities there might be in the world. So long as their rituals did not offend the rules of civil order and loyalty to the state, there was no bar to their worship.

The official cults

Although there is plenty of evidence for dedications to the whole of the Roman pantheon within provinces, special emphasis was placed upon the Capitoline triad of Jupiter, Juno and Minerva, since it was these three who were regarded as especially responsible for the continuing welfare of the Roman state. Such state gods, however, were not objects for private veneration but rather served public policy, and due regard paid to them on the part of a provincial was effectively a declaration of loyalty to Rome. This no doubt goes some of the way to explaining the temple to Neptune and Minerva dedicated on the authority of Cogidubnus at Chichester. Within the army Jupiter Optimus Maximus (Greatest and Best) occupied a similarly central role, with dedications renewed in January each year, as the many instances found at Maryport in Cumbria testify. By the time of the Claudian invasion, however, Rome had come to recognise that it had a potentially far more immediate and powerful focus for displays of loyalty in the person of the emperor himself. Deification of deceased emperors was already an established fact. Augustus had even gone so far as to allow non-citizens in Asia to dedicate sacred sites to himself in Pergamum and Nicomedia, thus extending to the Roman state the veneration of a living ruler that had long been practised by Eastern dynasts. That we hear of a Classical-style temple dedicated to Claudius in Colchester, therefore, comes as no surprise; neither does its association in the native mind with Roman oppression, making it in the early days of the Boudiccan rebellion a special object of loathing. Whether it was set up in Claudius' lifetime or was built under his successor, Nero, is in consequence unimportant. Nor were succeeding living emperors immune to veneration within Britain and other areas of the empire. If anything indeed it was the emperor of the day who stood at the heart of the imperial cult. True, the fiction of Romans not worshipping a living ruler was preserved by making dedications not so much to the man as to his *genius* or *numen*, his guiding spirit, thus reconciling Eastern practice with Roman susceptibilities - but such fine points are not likely to have meant much to the average native. Charged with funding the necessary rites of the imperial cult in the major conurbations were boards of six priests, the *Seviri Augustales*, drawn from the ranks of wealthy freedmen (ex-slaves). Among such men we hear of a Marcus Aurelius Lunaris, a *sevir* at both York and Lincoln, whose mercantile interests led him to dedicate an altar at Bordeaux. Another was Marcus Verecundius Diogenes, likewise a *sevir* at York. In addition to the central figures of the Roman pantheon there is also no shortage of references to other Roman deities: Apollo for instance, or Diana, Vulcan or Hercules. In some cases the dedication - be it an inscription or votive offering - may have overtones of a favour wanted or gratitude for a favour done. In other cases it may indicate personal devotion to a god associated with a profession, such as Asclepius, patron god of doctors, or Mercury, guardian of travellers and merchants.

In addition to the pantheon of Rome and the person of the emperor the Roman mind also reverenced personifications of abstract qualities such as discipline, virtue, victory, and fortune. Often these were associated with the emperor himself or mirrored the achievements of the times or official policy. This latter aspect especially explains the dedications to Discipline. Personifications of cities or whole areas might also attract veneration, whether it be Rome itself (the imperial cult in another guise perhaps) or parts of Britain: Brigantia, or individual locations with their peculiar *genii* or spirits.

Provincial deities of the West

The opening up of Britain to an influx of Roman cults merely continued a process that must have been a feature of every stage of Celtic migration into the island in the pre-Roman period. For this reason it is often difficult to tell whether a particular Celtic deity owes its presence here to the natural spread of Celtic culture, or was imported by auxiliary troops drawn from other Western provinces. Typical of the latter are the mother goddesses, who originated from the Rhine but whose area of influence was frequently extended by those making dedications, as inscriptions to the goddesses of Italy, Germany, Gaul and Britain found at Winchester, or those of Africa, Italy and Gaul found at York, make clear. Other Celtic gods of continental origin found in Britain include Lenus, who had a major shrine at Trier, the horse-goddess Epona, the *genii cucullati* - usually depicted as three standing figures wearing hooded cloaks - or Olludius from southern Gaul. In this grouping also may belong Anociticus (or in another spelling, Antenociticus) found at Benwell on Hadrian's Wall - unless his extremely restricted setting suggests a local god adopted by the garrison there.

More definite imports are those of German cults, though we have to admit the difficulty at times of distinguishing Celtic deities from German, except by reference to those who made the offerings to them. To this category, however, belong the Alaisiagae, to whom altars were set up at Housesteads by German auxiliaries from Twente in Holland, Garmangabis, to whom a dedication was made by Suebians at Lanchester, and perhaps Viradechthis and Ricagambeda venerated by Tungrians at Birrens.

Deities of the East

The expansion of the Roman empire from one end of the Mediterranean to the other brought with it the widespread dissemination of some cults whose exotic dogmas and ritual proved a powerful attraction for many. The agents of such movement were clearly those whose lifestyle was itself migratory, in particular the soldier and the merchant. Nor was the process restricted to the auxiliary forces of the army, who might be expected to trail the gods of their homeland after them from one posting to another. There is ample evidence of legionary personnel themselves becoming attached to the deities of areas in which they served at some stage in their careers. The Syrian cult of Dolichenus, for instance, who is usually identified with Jupiter, occurs in dedications set up by centurions in the military zone of Hadrian's Wall. In another example from Corbridge the god is linked both with Salus, goddess of safety, and thus of general appeal to soldiers, and with Caelestis Brigantia, herself a Severan conflation of a north African goddess and the personification of north Britain. Brigantia is found again at Birrens, but this time with attributes more usually associated with the Roman Minerva.

The northern frontier also provides evidence of dedications to Astarte, another north African goddess, Melkaart, the Hercules of Tyre, and Cybele, the great mother goddess of Asia Minor, whose priests dedicated themselves to her service through self-castration. Cybele also seems to have possessed a shrine in London, a city whose cosmopolitan populace made it a natural centre for a wide range of exotic cults. Here too we find reference to a shrine of the Egyptian goddess Isis scratched onto a jug, and to the shrine's repair by Marcus Martianius Pulcher when the ravages of time caused it to collapse. Small bronze figurines likewise attest to the cult of Osiris and Harpocrates, two other Egyptian gods, while Serapis - Osiris in a more Hellenised form - had a temple in York dedicated by the commander of the VI Victrix legion, Claudius Hieronymianus, as well as devotees in both Silchester and London. Among such divinities perhaps may also be included Bacchus, a member of the Greco-Roman pantheon, but whose associated mythology suggests an early Eastern origin, and whose orgiastic rites, like those associated with Cybele, promised release for emotional energies. As well as god of wine, Bacchus also operated on the level of a saviour god, a source of fertility and spiritual regeneration.

Mithraism

By far the most influential of the pagan Eastern cults that found their way to Britain was that of Mithras, an offshoot of Persian Zoroastrian beliefs or constellation-worship (scholary opinion is divided) and often conflated with the cult of the Unconquered Sun. His temples, are found in places as diverse as Carrawburgh, Rudchester and Housesteads on Hadrian's Wall, London, York and Caernarvon (with evidence for adherence to the cult at numerous other locations). While their relatively small dimensions suggest that this was never a numerically large religion, the social status of those attracted to it, both in military and civil life, gave it influence far beyond what might have been expected. Like other pagan cults it was tolerant of other gods, as shown by the range of sacred objects found in the vicinity of Mithraea. Unlike them, though, it was restricted to men, required and demanded from its devotees real commitment, a high moral standard of behaviour and, through its seven stages of initiation, considerable bravery - hence its appeal to army officers and merchants. The rise of Mithraism and the other exotic Eastern cults in Britain also coincided with a growth throughout the empire of a sense of spiritual anxiety, a search for communion with the divine and hence salvation, something that the state pantheon of Rome or the normal run of pagan religions never aimed to provide. In contrast to many other pagan cults where we know the name of the god, the location of the shrine and some aspects of the divinity's function through the dedicatory offerings made, yet remain ignorant of the adherent's actual beliefs concerning the god or the exact ritual involved, detail concerning Mithraism is much better documented. Essentially it was marked for the devotee by a spiritual journey from darkness to light, from death to eternal life, a mirror of its essentially dualistic nature based on the struggle within the universe between good, vested ultimately in the creator Ahura Mazda, and evil personified by Ariman. Somewhat surprisingly perhaps we find a dedication to the latter made by Volusius Irenaeus at York. Ariman, though, was not simply a Satan-figure, but rather a force in the world that man must struggle with to win salvation.

Central to Mithraism was the myth of the god's birth from rock or from a cosmic egg and his sacrifice of a great bull created by Ahura Mazda at the beginning of time. From the blood shed sprang all life on earth, the conversion of an act of destruction into one of creation. It is this that the surviving sculptural reliefs from the temples invariably depict: the young and energetic Mithras kneeling on the bull's back and plunging a dagger into the beast's neck, while on either side stand the attendants Cautes and Cautopates carrying torches, the one pointed to heaven, the other to earth, symbolising the dichotomy of light and dark, life and death. Just as the slaying of the bull was central to Mithraic belief, so Mithraism attempted to mirror in the structure of its temples the cave in which the central act was set. Some were actually built underground, those in Britain only partially so, but nevertheless they strove to exclude external light. Part of the ritual included a communal meal, a symbol of spiritual strengthening, and some participants wore masks appropriate to their grade of initiation: from the lowest Raven, through Bride, Soldier, Lion, Persian, Courier of the Sun, to the highest, Father. Adding to the overall theatrical effect of the ritual seems to have been use of artificial light at certain points in the ceremonies to illuminate the god's head with a halo, and a living burial to symbolise the initiate's passage through death to new life.

Many of the features of Mithraic belief have their parallels, of course, in that other great salvation religion of antiquity, Christianity. Such similarities indeed were to become a major cause of hostility between the two and seem ultimately to have led to the destruction of many Mithraic sites. At Carrawburgh, for instance, the temple suffered two periods of damage. The first was at the end of the third century, the other in the fourth. In London the early part of the fourth century saw major demolition of the Mithraeum, during or prior to which the important sculptural elements we now possess were hidden away. This was later followed by a period of reconstruction, but this time apparently for a different pagan cult. True, we have no direct evidence for the involvement of Christians in the destruction, but the balance of probability is weighted heavily in that direction.

Christianity

We do not know at what stage Christianity entered Britain, but the likelihood is that it came initially with merchants. Certainly, in its earliest period it was from the lower strata of society that the faith drew its main support, those on whom the promise of a blissful release from the world exerted a definite influence. In general, too, groups of early Christians were to be found where there were also concentrations of Jews. The earliest written evidence for its presence in Britain comes from Tertullian (c. AD 200) referring to the spread of the faith beyond the confines of the province, again suggesting the intervention of traders. By 314 on the other hand there were signs of an established hierarchy in the mention of three bishops, a priest and a deacon from Britain attending the Council of Arles. Partially filling in the intervening period is the evidence of archaeology, in particular the Water Newton treasure of mainly silver vessels and plaques dating from perhaps the third to the beginning of the fourth centuries, many of which bear Christian symbols and come from a properly constituted sanctuary. Significantly the form assumed by the silver-leaf plaques derives from a pattern more often found in pagan contexts, just as the dedication formula, 'Ancilla has fulfilled the vow she made', extends into a Christian setting what had long been a pagan practice. Other evidence is provided by the martyrdom of St. Alban, a soldier of Verulamium who gave himself up in place of a priest he sheltered. References to his judge as 'Caesar' make it possible that the events took place while the younger son of Septimius Severus was in charge of Britain, between AD 208-11. Others have suggested instead association with the persecutions that took place under Trajan Decius (AD 250-1) and Valerian (257-9), or that initiated by Diocletian in 303. From some accounts, though, this final burst of intolerance seems to have had little effect upon Britain, which by then was under the direct control of the western Caesar Constantius. The sources claim that his actions went no further than the demolition of buildings, but since these sources are themselves Christian and Constantius was the father of Constantine, the traditional champion of Christianity, we have to admit at least the possibility of doctored accounts. Lack of archaeological evidence for such destruction suggests in turn a proportionately small band of adherents. What fanned the flames of persecution was the refusal of Christians to accept that paganism, in particular the imperial cult, had any standing, and their attempts actually to spread this doctrine. As such, Christians were regarded as politically subversive, an enemy within.

With the final legalisation of Christianity under Constantine, followed by its positive encouragement under his successors, the faith probably began to make accelerated progress. Yet it would be wrong to see at this time a wholesale conversion of the country, especially since archaeology provides virtually no incontrovertible evidence for worship in urban centres, in sharp contrast to the continued use of pagan buildings. True, there is a shift to an east-west alignment of graves and a growing absence of grave goods at places like Dorchester, but whether the cause was Christian we cannot say. Nevertheless Britain continued to send delegations of clergy to later councils such as Rimini in 359, when British bishops accepted imperial subsidies to defray the cost of attendance. But is this evidence of the general poverty of the church in Britain or a sign of the bishops' attempt to avoid a council they thought might indulge in heresy?

The fourth century, however, did see the emergence of a class of Christians rich enough to embellish the living quarters of their country estates with mosaic floors and wall-paintings bearing Christian motifs, such as the Chi-Rho monogram at Lullingstone villa. Yet the continuing presence of pagan elements in such mosaics, now in the guise of Christian allegory, suggests the tenacity of earlier Classical forms. This helps to explain, for instance, the presence of Orpheus in a new context as the good shepherd at Woodchester and Barton Farm, or the use of Bellerophon slaying the Chimaera monster at Hinton St. Mary, Frampton and Lullingstone as a symbol of good overcoming evil.

In the fifth century the main evidence for Christianity in Britain comes from the activities of St. Germanus of Auxerre and his attempts in 429 and 446-7 to combat the spread of the Pelagian heresy which denied the need for God's grace in man's salvation and taught instead that men could achieve salvation by their own efforts. The picture that emerges is still, however, one of a relatively small-scale religion that had enjoyed favour in the fourth century but was now suffering from the same problems as afflicted the whole province. The evidence from cemeteries, baptismal fonts, engraved artefacts and personalia such as rings is easy to over-emphasise, especially when offerings continued to be made at pagan shrines. Even the mass baptisms conducted by St. Germanus before the Alleluia victory do not suggest a fully Christianised Britain.

It is an underlying assumption of this study of Romano-British religion so far that the dedications which form a vital element of evidence were made for the benefit of either the donor or those referred to. Not all inscriptions, however, were so benign, and the continuing discovery of curses, often inscribed on lead tablets and deliberately buried, provides evidence of attempts by individuals to settle scores for items stolen or other wrongs done. The lurid detail of divine retaliation sought, as in the case of one instance from London, 'I curse Tretia Maria and her life and mind and memory and liver and lungs mixed together...', indicates a considerable stream of venom that sought to mobilise the nether forces against an enemy.

Chapter 8
Romano-British Art

The art of a region is often a key to understanding its culture, and it seems appropriate, therefore, to conclude here with a brief chapter on the art of Roman Britain. This will not be a chapter on great works of Classical art, but is more concerned with the local productions of a province where Classical and native fused to produce something distinctive. Elegant artistic pieces in the Classical tradition have been found in Britain but they are usually, if not invariably, imported items such as the fine sculptures from the Walbrook Mithraeum in London, or the various pieces of busts and statues of emperors which doubtless had a significant influence on local production, but remain Roman rather than Romano-British. The influence of Classical art on British artistic production was profound, but what emerged in Britain during the Roman occupation was a distinctive blend of Roman and native which exploited the potential of the new technologies that became available and drew equally from Roman and native traditions. This brief account will be predominantly concerned with sculpture: it dominates because it is a durable, artistic medium which was exploited in all aspects of Romano-British life, military and civilian, secular and religious.

Painted decoration was common in wealthier houses and villas, but relatively little has survived. What has survived, notably from houses in Cirencester and Leicester, shows that at first wall painting in Roman Britain resembled closely the famous productions of the Romano-Campanian tradition, which is so fully represented by the wall paintings buried at Pompeii by the eruption of Vesuvius. Later, as is shown by the fourth century wall paintings of the villa at Lullingstone, painting in Britain had become part of the Romano-British tradition which had evolved by then.

Mosaics

Mosaics, too, were popular in Roman Britain, and there are many studies of them. In all respects mosaic was an imported medium. The very first mosaics in Britain were almost certainly the first century black and white mosaic designs which can be seen in the palace at Fishbourne, near Chichester. The palace was probably constructed for King Cogidubnus of the Atrebates, and it is believed that the artists who created the first pavements were imported from Italy. Certainly the designs of the Fishbourne mosaics bear a strong resemblance to those of contemporary mosaics at Ostia, the harbour town of Rome. By the second century the mosaic craft was well established in Britain, and British workmen were producing polychrome mosaic floors. The themes depicted tended to stick with very traditional Classical designs and subjects. The running *pelta* (shield) patterns and the intricately plaited guilloche borders of these pavements are part of an artistic vocabulary which was current throughout the Roman empire from one end to the other. The consistency of mosaic design may well be explained by assuming that pattern books were carried round by craftsmen who showed them to potential customers. By the end of the first century and thereafter better pavements contained figured scenes, often executed as *emblemata*, separate detailed panels worked by master craftsmen which were inserted into frames created by less skilled mosaicists.

The heyday of the Romano-British mosaicists came in the fourth century. The rich town house owners and especially the villa proprietors regularly commissioned large mosaic pavements on a scale which was grander than what was being attempted on the continent at the same time. Schools of mosaicists have been identified based on Cirencester, Dorchester and Water Newton. The Corinian school, based in Cirencester, was the most prolific of these workshops: its productions include the great pavement at Woodchester in Gloucestershire, which is reckoned to be the largest mosaic north of the Alps. Still in the fourth century the designs remained true to their Classical originals and were drawn almost exclusively from Classical mythology. Yet, the striking feature of the fourth century mosaics is the evidence they contain for the practice of Christianity in the province. Sometimes as in the Hinton St. Mary pavement which can be seen in the British Museum the mosaic is blatantly Christian. The pavement has a head of Christ set before an identifying

Chi-Rho symbol as its central emblema. The corners of the panel show figures which are descendants of the four winds, but they have lost their trumpets and it has been suggested that they are meant to be interpreted as the four evangelists. Other panels in the mosaic are less obviously Christian: on the four sides of the Christ panel are set scenes depicting the hunt, and the threshold leading into the room had a scene with Bellerophon killing the Chimaera. The last mentioned may be compared with later depictions of St. George killing the dragon and may be interpreted as showing the triumph of good forces over evil. The same scene was depicted in the villa at Lullingstone which contained a Christian chapel. A fourth school of mosaicists, known as the Petuarian school, was active in Yorkshire and Humberside. Its productions, such as the Venus pavement from Rudston, which may be compared with the Venus relief from High Rochester (Fig. 21), were less obviously Classicising than those of the other mosaic schools, and it could be argued that the provincial pieces produced by the Petuarian school were more genuinely Romano-British in style than those of the other schools.

Sculpture
Defining what is meant by the term 'Romano-British' (see ch. 1 above) is less of a problem when sculpture is being considered. Before the Roman occupation the art of Iron Age Britain consisted mainly of a tradition of complex decorative patterns, especially the beautiful flowing patterns, often referred to as La Tène designs which adorn metal items such as the bronze mirror from Birdlip. These Celtic designs continued to adorn metalwork throughout the Roman occupation, and it could reasonably be observed that they foreshadow the interlaces and pictorial designs which were such a feature of Anglo-Saxon art. That, of course, is another story, but it is interesting to see how in something as fundamental as artistic design the native traditions were partially submerged, but not completely drowned by the artistic forms of the invaders.

The other famous Iron Age tradition was the cult of the head. Celtic heads were potent religious totems, and they had a distinct stylistic tradition of their own which had profound influence on the art of Roman Britain. These heads were almost the only native sculptural productions: pre-Roman Britain was entirely lacking in sculptural relief. The features of the Celtic heads were remarkable: they displayed over-sized, staring, bulging eyes; long, straight noses; small, thin, downcast mouths. Hair could be reduced to swirling patterns not too far removed from the designs on bronzework. Their expressions were at once fierce and sad. Two heads, a male head from Gloucester (Fig. 17d) and a female head from Towcester (Fig. 17b) show how these motifs were adopted into the canon of Romano-British sculpture. The Gloucester head is a small sculpture, only 20 centimetres high; it was found at the site of the Bon Marché store in Northgate Street and is now in the Gloucester Museum. Though reduced to stylised patterns the hairstyle is recognisably Roman, and could easily have been influenced by military tombstones such as the funerary stele of the centurion Marcus Favonius Facilis in Colchester (Fig. 18) and the imperial portraits current in the first decades of the occupation. The prominent ears, too, bear a resemblance to Julio-Claudian portraits, though again they are reduced to stylised form. But other details are purely Celtic, especially the huge bulging eyes, the straight nose and the downcast slit of a mouth. The Julio-Claudian pointers place this piece early in the history of the occupation of Roman Britain, and it is fascinating to see how quickly British sculptors took up Classical ideas and merged them with their own traditions. The original context of this piece is unknown: it may just have been a detached bust, even a portrait bust, though that would be a very novel idea in Britain. But the vertical edge at the back of the neck makes it likely that the head was meant to be seen against a background and perhaps belonged to an architectural setting.

The female head from Towcester, however, clearly was designed as a separate bust. Although it also shows Celtic stylistic characteristics in respect of facial details, it has much of the feeling of the Classical tragic mask. Another head which demonstrates powerfully how Classical and Celtic traditions were merged productively is the head of the cult statue of Antenociticus (Fig. 17c) found in his temple at Benwell on Hadrian's Wall. The head has been broken from the body at the point where a bronze or gold torc encircled the neck. All the features are strongly Celtic, but the idea of a cult statue sculpted in the round is a Classical one, and in the quality and detail of its carving the piece has moved a long way forward from its Celtic predecessors. The hair is especially striking, combining a sense of a writhing Hellenistic profusion with the Celtic love of exaggerated design; and the particularly large locks which swirl to meet on the crown of the head above the centre line of the forehead almost suggest the horns which adorned some native deities.

The Roman army certainly brought to Britain sculptors who were responsible for producing inscriptions and tombstones. Although there was no native tradition of relief sculpture, the medium was grasped enthusiastically. Again it is surprising to see how quickly the fusion of Classical and native occurred. The Temple of Sulis-Minerva at Bath is thought to have been constructed in the first century AD. We are fortunate that the head of the cult statue, a beautiful gilt-bronze portrait of Minerva, has survived (Fig. 17a), as have fragments of the pedimental decoration of the main façade of the temple. The pediments showed tritons in the lower corners whilst in the main part of the triangular panel winged victories supported a huge roundel with laurel and oak leaves, at the centre of which is the head of a male Gorgon (Fig. 19). We do not know who the master sculptor who worked on this pediment was, but whoever produced this work was thoroughly aware of the conventions of Classical art and yet able to produce a head with all the wild potency of the Celtic tradition. The idea of having a sculpted pediment on the temple is purely Classical; Gorgon apart, the deities depicted are purely Classical; the very idea of a Gorgon with writhing, snaky hair is a Classical one. But what are we to make of this male (rather than female) creature with huge, staring eyes, long nose and grim mouth? This, in other words, is a triumph of the newly created Romano-British school: it is by any standards one of the greatest masterpieces of Roman provincial art.

Sculpture became the most common means of artistic expression in Roman Britain and was exploited for many purposes, religious and commemorative as well as decorative. The native deities were now depicted in the Roman medium of sculpted relief: thus we see triads of Celtic Mother Goddesses and the *genii cucullati* (Fig. 20) alongside such Classical visions as Venus bathing with her Nymphs (Fig. 21). The relief of Venus from High Rochester must be one of the most northerly of her manifestations. Classical versions were doubtless more flattering, but it is interesting to see how the story of Venus is understood well enough even beyond Hadrian's Wall, and the architectural framework in which the scene is depicted is also taken from the canons of Classical form, however debased these have become. The relief is another fine example of Roman provincial art.

Some pieces are highly personal, especially the wealth of tombstones that have survived. The tombstone of Aurelia Aureliana from Carlisle (Fig. 22) is one such. She is shown clutching a bunch of poppies, the symbol of sleep, and there are pine-cones on top of the frame of the monument. As large seeds the pine-cones symbolised life, and the optimistic message of this tombstone is clear: Aurelia is not dead, only sleeping, and there is a promise of life to come. The piece thus reflects the fact that it was carved in the third century when the Roman empire was not at its healthiest, but the religious impact of Christianity was becoming more and more apparent. The tombstone of Aurelia may have been meant for a portrait, but the facial features are not distinctive, and the *Birrus Britannicus* which she wears stops at the knee. Female figures are more normally depicted with ankle-length garments, and one is left to wonder whether this piece was originally intended for a man, but bought 'off the peg' by Aurelia's widower. The point is important because it underlines the observation that this sort of sculpture was not entirely the prerogative of the richer upper classes. Aurelia was a freedwoman, who was valued enough by her perhaps not-so-wealthy husband that he had a stone erected for her. This tombstone, in other words, is truly Romano-British, and serves to show how by the third century there was a real interpenetration of cultures even on the furthest boundary of the province.

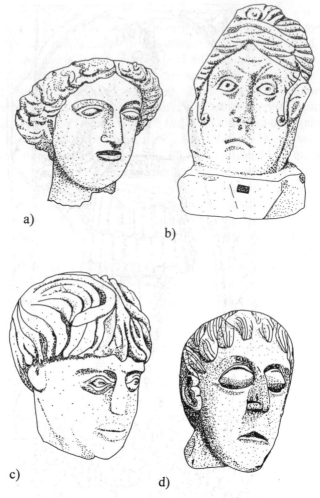

Fig. 17   a) Gilt-bronze head of cult statue of Minerva, from the
temple of Sulis-Minerva at Bath.
b) Female head from Towcester.
c) Head of cult statue of Antenociticus from the temple at
Benwell on Hadrian's Wall.
d) Male head found at Northgate Street, Gloucester.

Fig. 18   Tombstone of the centurion Marcus Favonius Facilis from Colchester.

Fig. 19   Roundel showing male Gorgon from the pediment of the temple of Sulis-Minerva at Bath.

Fig. 20   Relief of Genii Cucullati from Netherby (Cumberland).

Fig. 21   Sculpted relief of Venus bathing and attendant Nymphs from High Rochester.

Fig. 22   Tombstone of Aurelia Aureliana from Carlisle.

Suggestions for Further Study

1. The narratives of Roman involvement in Britain given by Caesar and Tacitus are suffused with an impression of objectivity. Is this justified?
2. Was the Boudiccan rebellion inevitable, and what does it tell us of Roman attitudes to the provincial population?
3. Many of the sources point to the third-century usurpers in Britain as either being fools or cool and calculating. Is there a case instead for claiming that they were at times forced into assuming imperial honours by external pressures?
4. Despite the problems that Britain faced in the fourth century the Roman hold scarcely seems to have wavered until it collapsed in the early years of the fifth century. Were external pressures or internal dissent the real cause of the breakdown?
5. Much of Romano-British military history appears dominated by a quest for holdable frontiers. Did the Romans ever succeed in finding an answer to the problem?
6. At times the administration of Roman Britain seems like a cobbling together of elements that lack a coherent structure. Is this a correct assessment?
7. Is it sensible to conclude that the establishment of large numbers of cities was the key factor in securing stability in the Roman province of Britain?
8. Were villas in Roman Britain more like hunting lodges for the wealthy or productive working farms?
9. Despite the large number of religious dedications from the Roman period found in Britain, we still know relatively little of the religious life of the province. Why is this?
10. Does Romano-British art demonstrate that there was a real fusion of Classical and native culture during the Roman occupation of Britain?

Suggestions for Further Reading

1. Original sources in translation

Caesar, *The Conquest of Gaul*, translated by S. A. Handford, 2nd edition revised with a new introduction by A. R. Burn (Penguin, 1972).

Tacitus, *The Agricola and the Germania*, translated by H. Mattingly, 2nd edition (Penguin 1970).

S. Ireland, *Roman Britain, a Sourcebook* (2nd edition, Routledge, 1996).

2. Modern works

J. Alcock, *English Heritage Book of Life in Roman Britain* (Tempus, 1998). An excellent collection of information on social life.

P. T. Bidwell, *English Heritage Book of Roman Forts in Britain* (Batsford, 1997). This is a very useful digest of Roman forts in all their guises.

R. Birley, *Vindolanda, a Fort on Hadrian's Wall* (Thames & Hudson, 1977). This remains the basic exposition of a unique site.

A. K. Bowman, *Life and Letters of the Roman Frontier* (British Museum, 1994). In recent times Vindolanda has revealed the remains of some fascinating letters illustrating life on the northern frontier. Bowman's treatment of them and their contents helps to bring their writers to life.

D. Breeze, *Roman Scotland: Frontier Country* (Batsford, 1996). A thorough analysis of the Roman hold on Scotland.

J. Burke, *Roman England* (Artus, 1993). This book is useful for its at times stunning illustrations.

B. Burnham and J. Wacher, *The 'Small Towns' of Roman Britain* (Batsford 1990). This is a very thorough study of the less grand urban establishments which were such an important aspect of the Romanisation of Britain.

P. A. Clayton, *A Companion to Roman Britain* (Phaidon, 1980). An encyclopaedic work with chapters by eminent scholars on topics such as social organisation, the people of Roman Britain, Christianity, the economy, and the end of Roman Britain.

J. Crow, *The English Heritage Book of Housesteads* (Batsford, 1995). This work does full justice to what is arguably the most famous of the forts on Hadrian's Wall.

P. Crummy, *City of Victory: the Story of Colchester – Britain's First Roman Town* (Coclchester, 1997). A lavishly illustrated guide to Britain's first capital city.

B. Cunliffe, *Fishbourne Roman Palace* (Tempus, 1998). A detailed guide to what is arguably Roman Britain's most famous building.

G. de la Bédoyère, *The Finds of Roman Britain* (Batsford, 1989). This offers thorough and well illustrated accounts of the artefacts found on archaeological sites and what they can tell us.

G. de la Bédoyère, *The Buildings of Roman Britain* (Batsford, 1991). This provides an extremely well illustrated and useful survey of the buildings found at Romano-British sites and what they originally looked like.

G. de la Bédoyère, *English Heritage Book of Roman Towns in Britain* (Batsford, 1992). This offers a thorough survey of most aspects of urban life and development.

G. de la Bédoyère, *Hadrian's Wall: History and Guide* (Tempus, 1998). A handy guide to the northern frontier.

G. de la Bédoyère, *English Heritage Book of Roman Villas and the Countryside* (Batsford, 1993). This is a very readable and well illustrated account of this important aspect of Roman Britain.

S. Frere, *Britannia* (3rd edition, Routledge & Kegan Paul, 1987). Although superseded in part by Salway, this remains a remarkably balanced account of Roman Britain.

W. T. Hanson, *Agricola and the Conquest of the North* (Batsford, 1989). This detailed account helps us to understand what was going on in this period of rapid movement and expansion.

M. Henig, *Religion in Roman Britain* (2nd edition, Batsford, 1995). This is a scholarly, authoritative, but very readable, account of this subject.

M. Henig, *The Art of Roman Britain* (Batsford, 1995). This important book provides useful account of many aspects of this subject.

S. Johnson, *English Heritage Book of Hadrian's Wall* (Batsford, 1989). This is a lavishly illustrated and clear description of the northern frontier.

B. Jones & D. Mattingly, *An Atlas of Roman Britain* (Blackwell, 1990). This usefully combines a wealth of maps, diagrams and illustrations with helpful text on the conquest and development of the province, the economy, countryside and religion.

M. Millett, *English Heritage Book of Roman Britain* (Batsford, 1995). This overview of the province continues the tradition in the English Heritage series of combining lavish illustration with understandable text, and puts the Roman occupation of Britain into its broader context.

G. Milne, *The Port of Roman London* (Batsford, 1985). The author brings to life recent discoveries in the most important port of Roman Britain.

P. Ottaway, *Roman York* (London, 1993). This is an outstanding presentation of one of the province's most significant cities.

T. W. Potter & C. Johns, *Roman Britain* (British Museum, 1992). This provides an easily digested survey of the province.

P. Salway, *Roman Britain* (2nd edition, Oxford, 1982). This is the fullest available account of virtually every aspect of Roman Britain.

P. Salway, *The Oxford Illustrated History of Roman Britain* (Oxford, 1993). This combines the thoroughness of Salway's previous work with some useful illustrations.

C. Thomas, *Christianity in Roman Britain to AD 500* (Batsford, 1981). This is an extremely scholarly study of this subject.

M. Todd, *Roman Britain, 55BC-AD200* (2nd edition London, 1997). The volume provides a useful survey of the Roman presence in Britain.

J. Wacher, *The Towns of Roman Britain* (2nd edition, Batsford, 1995). For anyone wanting to explore the detail of the urban development in Roman Britain this is essential.

R. White and P. Barker, Wroxeter, *Life and Death of a Roman City* (Tempus 1998). This provides a fascinating insight into the growth and decline of one of Roman Britain's largest cities.

In addition to the volumes listed above, those who want a deeper understanding of the tribes and peoples who inhabited Roman Britain may be interested to consult the following books:

K. Branigan, *The Catuvellauni* (Sutton, 1985).

B. Cunliffe, *The Regni* (Duckworth, 1973).

A. Detsicas, *The Cantiaci* (Sutton, 1983).

R. Dunnett, *The Trinovantes* ((Duckworth, 1975).

B. Hartley and L. Fitts, *The Brigantes* (Sutton, 1988).

H. Higham and B. Jones, *The Carvetii* (Sutton, 1985).

H. Ramm, *The Parisi* (Duckworth, 1978).

M. Todd, *The Coritani* (Duckworth, 1973).

G. Webster, *The Cornovii* (Duckworth, 1975).

Index